This book belongs to

_____

Hey you!

Are you ready for some fun and laughter while learning about Jesus Christ? This book is full of silly jokes that will make you laugh and teach you amazing things about Jesus!

A long time ago, Jesus was a very special person who did incredible things. He was the Son of God, which means He came from God to show us how to love and be kind. Jesus taught us all about being nice to others, saying sorry when we make mistakes, and forgiving people who hurt us. He even did some awesome miracles, like healing sick people and turning water into wine!

In this book, you'll find jokes about Jesus' adventures, His friends, and the cool things He did. You can read these jokes by yourself, tell them to your friends, or even use them to play fun games.

Get ready to laugh and learn about Jesus in a super fun way! Let's dive into the fun!

Table of Content

Conclusion

Joke Formats

Knock-knock jokes

Punny jokes

Riddle jokes

One-liner jokes

PART ONE

Jesus' Life and Teachings

CHAPTER ONE

BIRTH AND CHILDHOOD

Knock, knock.

Who's there?

Shepherds.

Shepherds who?

Shepherds watching their flocks by night—until the angels showed up!

Anecdote: Shepherds were the first to hear the good news of Jesus' birth from angels.

Verse: "And there were shepherds living out in the fields nearby, keeping watch over their flocks at night." (Luke 2:8)

Knock, knock.
Who's there?
Angel.
Angel who?
Angel Gabriel! I've got good news—Mary's having a baby!

Anecdote: *The angel Gabriel announced to Mary that she would give birth to Jesus.*
Verse: *"The angel went to her and said, 'Greetings, you who are highly favored! The Lord is with you.'" (Luke 1:28)*

Knock, knock.
Who's there?
Gold.
Gold who?
Gold, frankincense, and myrrh—it's the wise men!

Anecdote: *The wise men brought gifts of gold, frankincense, and myrrh to honor Jesus.*
Verse: *"On coming to the house, they saw the child with his mother Mary, and they bowed down and worshiped him. Then they opened their treasures and presented him with gifts." (Matthew 2:11)*

Knock, knock.
Who's there?
Bethlehem.

Bethlehem who?

Bethlehem Inn—sorry, we're all booked!

Anecdote: Mary and Joseph couldn't find room at the inn when they arrived in Bethlehem.

Verse: "She gave birth to her firstborn, a son. She wrapped him in cloths and placed him in a manger, because there was no guest room available for them." (Luke 2:7)

Knock, knock.

Who's there?

Star.

Star who?

Star of Bethlehem—follow me to the newborn King!

Anecdote: The star led the wise men to the place where Jesus was born.

Verse: "We saw his star when it rose and have come to worship him." (Matthew 2:2)

Knock, knock.

Who's there?

Manger.

Manger who?

Manger glad you found a place to stay?

Anecdote: Jesus was laid in a manger because there was no room for His family in the inn.

Verse: *"She wrapped him in cloths and placed him in a manger." (Luke 2:7)*

Knock, knock.
Who's there?
Census.
Census who?
Census says Joseph and Mary had to travel all the way to Bethlehem!

Anecdote: *Joseph and Mary went to Bethlehem because of the Roman census.*
Verse: *"So Joseph also went up from the town of Nazareth in Galilee to Judea, to Bethlehem the town of David, because he belonged to the house and line of David." (Luke 2:4)*

Knock, knock.
Who's there?
Herod.
Herod who?
Herod it through the grapevine—there's a new King in town!

Anecdote: *King Herod was disturbed by news of Jesus' birth, seeing Him as a threat to his rule.*
Verse: *"When King Herod heard this he was disturbed, and all Jerusalem with him." (Matthew 2:3)*

Knock, knock.
Who's there?
Nazareth.
Nazareth who?
Nazareth—you mean nothing good can come from here? Just wait until you meet Jesus!

Anecdote: Jesus grew up in Nazareth, a small town with a humble reputation.
Verse: "Nazareth! Can anything good come from there?" Nathanael asked. "Come and see," said Philip. (John 1:46)

Knock, knock.
Who's there?
Baby.
Baby who?
Baby Jesus! Wrapped in swaddling clothes and ready to save the world.

Anecdote: Jesus was born as a baby to fulfill the prophecy of the Messiah.
Verse: "Today in the town of David a Savior has been born to you; he is the Messiah, the Lord." (Luke 2:11)

Punny Jokes

Joke: Why did the shepherds bring their sheep to Jesus' birth?
Punchline: Because they wanted to "ewe-phorically" celebrate the Lamb of God!

Anecdote: Shepherds were the first to visit baby Jesus, symbolizing His future role as the Good Shepherd.
Verse: "The shepherds said to one another, 'Let's go to Bethlehem and see this thing that has happened, which the Lord has told us about.'" (Luke 2:15)

Joke: Why did Mary and Joseph avoid the local bakeries in Bethlehem?
Punchline: Because they already had the "bread of life" in the manger!

Anecdote: Jesus' humble birth in a manger shows that He is the spiritual nourishment for all mankind.
Verse: "I am the bread of life. Whoever comes to me will never go hungry." (John 6:35)

Joke: Why didn't the wise men ever argue on their way to Bethlehem?
Punchline: Because they always followed the "bright" idea!

Anecdote: The wise men followed the star to find the newborn Jesus, showing their devotion and wisdom.
Verse: "We saw his star when it rose and have come to worship him." (Matthew 2:2)

Joke: What's Mary's favorite workout routine?
Punchline: "Carrying the weight" of the world!

Anecdote: Mary was chosen to bear Jesus, who would carry the weight of humanity's sins.
Verse: "The virgin will conceive and give birth to a son, and they will call him Immanuel (which means 'God with us')." (Matthew 1:23)

Joke: Why didn't Joseph build a better crib for baby Jesus?
Punchline: He figured a "manger" was already "stable" enough!

Anecdote: Baby Jesus was placed in a manger, a feeding trough, emphasizing His humble beginnings.
Verse: "She wrapped him in cloths and placed him in a manger." (Luke 2:7)

Joke: Why did the angels sing at Jesus' birth?

Punchline: Because they wanted to "hark" out the good news!

Anecdote: A choir of angels announced Jesus' birth to shepherds, praising God for the coming of the Savior.
Verse: "Suddenly a great company of the heavenly host appeared with the angel, praising God." (Luke 2:13)

Joke: Why did the wise men bring gold, frankincense, and myrrh?
Punchline: Because gift cards hadn't been invented yet!

Anecdote: The wise men brought valuable gifts to honor Jesus, each with deep spiritual meaning.
Verse: "Then they opened their treasures and presented him with gifts of gold, frankincense, and myrrh." (Matthew 2:11)

Joke: What did the innkeeper say when Joseph asked for a room?
Punchline: "Sorry, we're fully 'booked,' but you can 'manger' in the stable!"

Anecdote: Joseph and Mary couldn't find room in the inn, so they had to stay in a stable, where Jesus was born.
Verse: "She wrapped him in cloths and placed him in a manger, because there was no guest room available for them." (Luke 2:7)

Joke: Why did baby Jesus stay so calm in the manger?
Punchline: He knew He was in "stable" hands!

Anecdote: *Jesus' peaceful birth in a humble manger reflects His role as the Prince of Peace.*

Verse: *"For to us a child is born, to us a son is given... and he will be called Prince of Peace." (Isaiah 9:6)*

Joke: What's the first thing baby Jesus learned?

Punchline: To "love thy swaddling clothes" as thyself!

Anecdote: *Jesus was wrapped in swaddling clothes, a symbol of His humanity and connection to all people.*

Verse: *"She gave birth to her firstborn, a son. She wrapped him in cloths and placed him in a manger." (Luke 2:7)*

One liners

Joke: Jesus was born in a stable—talk about a "low-key" entrance for a King!

Anecdote: *Jesus was born in a humble stable, symbolizing His humility and accessibility to all.*

Verse: *"She wrapped him in cloths and placed him in a manger, because there was no guest room available for them." (Luke 2:7)*

Joke: The wise men brought gifts of gold, frankincense, and myrrh—guess they skipped the baby registry!

Anecdote: The Magi presented symbolic gifts that foreshadowed Jesus' kingship and sacrifice.
Verse: "They opened their treasures and presented him with gifts: gold, frankincense, and myrrh." (Matthew 2:11)

Joke: Shepherds were the first to hear about Jesus—because even the angels knew they'd be "flocking" to see Him!

Anecdote: The angels appeared to the shepherds, announcing the birth of Christ.
Verse: "The angel said to them, 'Do not be afraid. I bring you good news that will cause great joy for all the people.'" (Luke 2:10)

Joke: Mary didn't need a fancy hospital—she knew that the best things come in mangers!

Anecdote: Jesus was born in a simple manger, underscoring the humble circumstances of His birth.
Verse: "She gave birth to her firstborn, a son... and placed him in a manger." (Luke 2:7)

Joke: Bethlehem was so crowded, Mary and Joseph were probably just happy they didn't end up on the street—literally!

Anecdote: *Mary and Joseph couldn't find room at the inn and had to stay in a stable.*
Verse: *"There was no guest room available for them." (Luke 2:7)*

Joke: The star of Bethlehem was so bright, even the wise men didn't need Google Maps to find their way!

Anecdote: *The star guided the wise men from the East to the place where Jesus was born.*
Verse: *"The star they had seen when it rose went ahead of them until it stopped over the place where the child was." (Matthew 2:9)*

Joke: King Herod heard about a new King being born, and he immediately thought, "Well, this is awkward."

Anecdote: *Herod saw Jesus' birth as a threat to his throne and sought to kill Him.*
Verse: *"When King Herod heard this, he was disturbed, and all Jerusalem with him." (Matthew 2:3)*

Joke: Mary and Joseph had the ultimate road trip to Bethlehem—except the donkey didn't have air conditioning!

Anecdote: *Joseph and Mary traveled to Bethlehem for the Roman census, fulfilling prophecy.*
Verse: *"So Joseph also went up from the town of Nazareth... to Bethlehem." (Luke 2:4)*

Joke: Jesus was born in Bethlehem, and suddenly, the little town became "the birthplace of the Savior" on TripAdvisor!

Anecdote: *Bethlehem, though small, became the birthplace of Jesus, fulfilling Old Testament prophecy.*
Verse: *"But you, Bethlehem, though you are small... out of you will come a ruler." (Micah 5:2)*

Joke: The angels sang at Jesus' birth, and I guess you could say they had the "heavenly" top of the charts!

Anecdote: *The angels praised God and proclaimed peace to those on whom His favor rests.*
Verse: *"Suddenly a great company of the heavenly host appeared... praising God." (Luke 2:13-14)*

Riddles

Riddle: I'm small and humble, yet a King was born within me. What am I?

Answer: Bethlehem!

Anecdote: *Bethlehem, a small town, became the birthplace of Jesus, fulfilling prophecy.*
Verse: *"But you, Bethlehem... out of you will come a ruler." (Micah 5:2)*

Riddle: I have no room for a King, yet He was born under my roof. What am I?
Answer: The inn in Bethlehem!

Anecdote: *There was no room in the inn for Mary and Joseph, so Jesus was born in a stable.*
Verse: *"There was no guest room available for them." (Luke 2:7)*

Riddle: I shine brightly in the sky and led wise men from afar. What am I?
Answer: The Star of Bethlehem!

Anecdote: *The star led the wise men to the place where Jesus was born.*
Verse: *"We saw his star when it rose and have come to worship him." (Matthew 2:2)*

Riddle: I announced the birth of a King, but I'm not a messenger. I'm part of a song. What am I?
Answer: The angels!

Anecdote: *The angels appeared to shepherds to announce the birth of Jesus, praising God.*
Verse: *"A great company of the heavenly host appeared, praising God." (Luke 2:13)*

Riddle: I'm not a throne, but I held the newborn King. What am I?

Answer: A manger!

Anecdote: Jesus was laid in a manger after His birth, showing His humble beginnings.
Verse: "She wrapped him in cloths and placed him in a manger." (Luke 2:7)

Riddle: I traveled from afar, following a star, and I brought gifts. Who am I?

Answer: The wise men!

Anecdote: The wise men brought gifts of gold, frankincense, and myrrh to honor baby Jesus.
Verse: "On coming to the house... they presented him with gifts of gold, frankincense, and myrrh." (Matthew 2:11)

Riddle: I'm known as "God with us," and I came as a baby. Who am I?

Answer: Immanuel!

Anecdote: Immanuel means "God with us," a title for Jesus, emphasizing His divine presence among us.
Verse: "They will call him Immanuel (which means 'God with us')." (Matthew 1:23)

Riddle: I am a royal ruler, but when I heard about a newborn King, I felt threatened. Who am I?

Answer: King Herod!

Anecdote: *King Herod feared that the birth of Jesus would threaten his rule, leading him to plot against the baby.*
Verse: *"When King Herod heard this, he was disturbed, and all Jerusalem with him."* *(Matthew 2:3)*

Riddle: I am a carpenter, but my most important job was raising the Son of God. Who am I?
Answer: Joseph!

Anecdote: *Joseph, though a carpenter, was chosen by God to be the earthly father of Jesus.*
Verse: *"Joseph... took Mary home as his wife."* *(Matthew 1:24)*

Riddle: I traveled with my pregnant wife on a long journey to fulfill a census. Who am I?
Answer: Joseph!

Anecdote: *Joseph took Mary to Bethlehem to register for the Roman census, fulfilling prophecy.*
Verse: *"Joseph also went up from Nazareth to Bethlehem... to register."* *(Luke 2:4-5)*

CHAPTER TWO

MINISTRIES AND MIRACLES

Knock, knock.

Who's there?

Fish.

Fish who?

Fish you catch men like Jesus does!

Anecdote: Jesus called His disciples to be "fishers of men," encouraging them to bring people to God.

Verse: "Come, follow me," Jesus said, "and I will send you out to fish for people." (Matthew 4:19)

Knock, knock.
Who's there?
Loaves.
Loaves who?
Loaves and fishes—enough to feed 5,000!

Anecdote: Jesus miraculously fed 5,000 people with just five loaves of bread and two fish.
Verse: "Taking the five loaves and the two fish and looking up to heaven, he gave thanks and broke the loaves." (Matthew 14:19)

Knock, knock.
Who's there?
Water.
Water who?
Water you doing? Just walking on it like Jesus!

Anecdote: Jesus walked on water, showing His authority over nature.
Verse: "Shortly before dawn, Jesus went out to them, walking on the lake." (Matthew 14:25)

Knock, knock.
Who's there?
Wine.
Wine who?
Wine not turn water into me, like Jesus did?

Anecdote: Jesus' first miracle was turning water into wine at a wedding in Cana.

Verse: "Jesus said to the servants, 'Fill the jars with water'; so they filled them to the brim." (John 2:7)

Knock, knock.
Who's there?
Lazarus.
Lazarus who?
Lazarus—back from the dead, thanks to Jesus!

Anecdote: Jesus raised Lazarus from the dead, displaying His power over life and death.
Verse: "Jesus called in a loud voice, 'Lazarus, come out!' The dead man came out." (John 11:43-44)

Knock, knock.
Who's there?
Blind.
Blind who?
Blind no more—Jesus gave me sight!

Anecdote: Jesus healed a blind man, allowing him to see again.
Verse: "Jesus said, 'Go, your faith has healed you.' Immediately he received his sight." (Mark 10:52)

Knock, knock.
Who's there?
Storm.

Storm who?

Storm's over—Jesus just told it to "be still"!

Anecdote: Jesus calmed a violent storm while on a boat with His disciples, showing His power over the weather.
Verse: "He got up, rebuked the wind and said to the waves, 'Quiet! Be still!' Then the wind died down and it was completely calm." (Mark 4:39)

Knock, knock.
Who's there?
Demons.
Demons who?
Demons who ran away when Jesus came around!

Anecdote: Jesus cast out demons from many people, including the man possessed by a legion of demons.
Verse: "For Jesus had commanded the impure spirit to come out of the man." (Luke 8:29)

Knock, knock.
Who's there?
Paralyzed.
Paralyzed who?
Paralyzed no more—Jesus told me to get up and walk!

Anecdote: Jesus healed a paralyzed man, instructing him to take up his mat and walk.
Verse: "Then Jesus said to him, 'Get up! Pick up your mat and walk.'" (John 5:8)

Knock, knock.
Who's there?
Leper.
Leper who?
Leper you know, Jesus healed me and I'm clean now!

Anecdote: Jesus healed a man with leprosy, restoring his health.
Verse: "Jesus reached out his hand and touched the man. 'I am willing,' he said. 'Be clean!' Immediately he was cleansed of his leprosy." (Matthew 8:3)

Punny Jokes

Joke: Why did the fish attend Jesus' sermon?
A: Because it heard there was plenty of "soul" food!

Anecdote: Jesus fed 5,000 people with just five loaves and two fish, showing He could satisfy both spiritual and physical hunger.
Verse: "Taking the five loaves and the two fish and looking up to heaven, he gave thanks and broke the loaves." (Matthew 14:19)

Joke: Why did Jesus always win at hide and seek?
A: Because even the blind could see He was the Light of the world!

Anecdote: Jesus healed the blind, showing His ability to open both physical and spiritual eyes to the truth.
Verse: "I am the light of the world. Whoever follows me will never walk in darkness, but will have the light of life." (John 8:12)

Joke: Why don't storms mess with Jesus?
Because He can always tell them to "wave" goodbye!

Anecdote: Jesus calmed the storm while His disciples were afraid, demonstrating His power over nature.
Verse: "He got up, rebuked the wind and said to the waves, 'Quiet! Be still!' Then the wind died down and it was completely calm." (Mark 4:39)

Joke: Why was Lazarus good at parties?
A: Because he really knew how to make a comeback!

Anecdote: Jesus raised Lazarus from the dead, showing His authority over life and death.
Verse: "Jesus called in a loud voice, 'Lazarus, come out!' The dead man came out." (John 11:43-44)

Joke: Why didn't the water at the wedding feel left out?
A: Because Jesus turned it into something "grape"!

Anecdote: Jesus performed His first miracle at a wedding in Cana, turning water into wine.

Verse: *"Jesus said to the servants, 'Fill the jars with water'; so they filled them to the brim." (John 2:7)*

Joke: Why did the bread get promoted in Jesus' miracle?
A: Because it "rose" to the occasion!

Anecdote: *Jesus multiplied loaves of bread to feed thousands, showing His power to provide abundantly.*
Verse: *"They all ate and were satisfied, and the disciples picked up twelve basketfuls of broken pieces that were left over." (Matthew 14:20)*

Joke: Why did the fig tree get into trouble with Jesus?
A: Because it was "leafing" out of its responsibilities!

Anecdote: *Jesus cursed a fig tree for being fruitless, using it as a lesson about the importance of spiritual fruitfulness.*
Verse: *"Seeing a fig tree by the road, he went up to it but found nothing on it except leaves. Then he said to it, 'May you never bear fruit again!'" (Matthew 21:19)*

Joke: Why did the paralyzed man walk confidently?
A: Because Jesus gave him a "leg up"!

Anecdote: *Jesus healed a paralyzed man, telling him to pick up his mat and walk, demonstrating His power to heal.*
Verse: *"Then Jesus said to him, 'Get up! Pick up your mat and walk.'" (John 5:8)*

Joke: Why did the demons tremble when they saw Jesus?

A: Because they knew He was the real "exorcising" authority!

Anecdote: *Jesus cast out demons from many people, including a man possessed by a legion of demons.*

Verse: *"For Jesus had commanded the impure spirit to come out of the man." (Luke 8:29)*

Joke: Why did the disciples trust Jesus to walk on water?

A: Because He knew how to "stay afloat" in any situation!

Anecdote: *Jesus walked on water to reach His disciples, showing His power over the natural world.*

Verse: *"Shortly before dawn Jesus went out to them, walking on the lake." (Matthew 14:25)*

One Liner Jokes

Joke: Jesus fed 5,000 two fish—talk about a "bread-winning" miracle!

Anecdote: *Jesus multiplied a small amount of food to feed a massive crowd, demonstrating His ability to provide.*

Verse: *"Taking the five loaves and the two fish and looking up to heaven, he gave thanks and broke the loaves." (Matthew 14:19)*

Joke: Jesus walked on water because when you're the Son of God, you never "sink" to ordinary levels!

Anecdote: *Jesus walked on water to reach His disciples, proving His authority over the natural world.*
Verse: *"Shortly before dawn Jesus went out to them, walking on the lake." (Matthew 14:25)*

Joke: Lazarus was dead for four days, but thanks to Jesus, he had the best "comeback" story ever!

Anecdote: *Jesus raised Lazarus from the dead, showing His power over life and death.*
Verse: *"Jesus called in a loud voice, 'Lazarus, come out!' The dead man came out." (John 11:43-44)*

Joke: Jesus turned water into wine—proof that with Him, life is always a celebration!

Anecdote: *At the wedding in Cana, Jesus performed His first miracle by turning water into wine.*
Verse: *"Jesus said to the servants, 'Fill the jars with water'; so they filled them to the brim." (John 2:7)*

Joke: When Jesus told the storm to calm down, even the weather knew not to "wave" back at Him!

Anecdote: *Jesus calmed a storm while on a boat with His disciples, showing His authority over nature.*
Verse: *"He got up, rebuked the wind and said to the waves, 'Quiet! Be still!' Then the wind died down and it was completely calm." (Mark 4:39)*

Joke: The blind could see after meeting Jesus, because with Him, there's always "clarity"!

Anecdote: *Jesus healed the blind, giving them sight and spiritual understanding.*
Verse: *"Jesus said, 'Go, your faith has healed you.' Immediately he received his sight." (Mark 10:52)*

Joke: When Jesus cast out demons, they didn't "stick around"—they ran for the hills!

Anecdote: *Jesus cast out demons from a man, displaying His power over evil spirits.*
Verse: *"For Jesus had commanded the impure spirit to come out of the man." (Luke 8:29)*

Joke: Jesus healed the paralyzed man—talk about someone who got a real "leg up" on life!

Anecdote: *Jesus healed a paralyzed man, allowing him to walk again.*

Verse: *"Then Jesus said to him, 'Get up! Pick up your mat and walk.'" (John 5:8)*

Joke: The fig tree didn't bear fruit, so Jesus gave it some "tough love"—it withered away!

Anecdote: *Jesus cursed a fig tree for not bearing fruit, using it as a lesson on spiritual fruitfulness.*

Verse: *"Seeing a fig tree by the road, he went up to it but found nothing on it except leaves. Then he said to it, 'May you never bear fruit again!'" (Matthew 21:19)*

Joke: When Jesus healed the lepers, they were "clean" in no time—no soap required!

Anecdote: *Jesus healed those with leprosy, cleansing them of the disease.*

Verse: *"Jesus reached out his hand and touched the man. 'I am willing,' he said. 'Be clean!' Immediately he was cleansed of his leprosy." (Matthew 8:3)*

Riddle Jokes

Riddle: I can't swim, but I walked across water. Who am I?
Answer: Jesus!

Anecdote: *Jesus walked on water to reach His disciples, demonstrating His authority over nature.*

Verse: *"Shortly before dawn Jesus went out to them, walking on the lake." (Matthew 14:25)*

Riddle: I started out as water but ended up being the life of the party. What am I?

Answer: Wine!

Anecdote: *Jesus turned water into wine at the wedding in Cana, performing His first recorded miracle.*

Verse: *"Jesus said to the servants, 'Fill the jars with water'; so they filled them to the brim." (John 2:7)*

Riddle: I was once blind but now can see, thanks to the touch of the one who is light. Who am I?

Answer: The blind man healed by Jesus!

Anecdote: *Jesus healed several blind individuals, granting them physical and spiritual sight.*

Verse: *"Jesus said, 'Go, your faith has healed you.' Immediately he received his sight." (Mark 10:52)*

Riddle: I was dead for four days, but Jesus called me back to life. Who am I?

Answer: Lazarus!

Anecdote: *Jesus raised Lazarus from the dead, showcasing His power over life and death.*

Verse: *"Jesus called in a loud voice, 'Lazarus, come out!' The dead man came out."* *(John 11:43-44)*

Riddle: I was carried in through the roof, but I walked out on my own two feet. Who am I?

Answer: The paralyzed man!

Anecdote: *Jesus healed a paralyzed man whose friends lowered him through a roof to reach Jesus.*

Verse: *"Jesus said to the paralyzed man, 'I tell you, get up, take your mat and go home.'"* *(Luke 5:24)*

Riddle: I was a small lunch for one, but I fed thousands when blessed by the Son. What am I?

Answer: Five loaves and two fish!

Anecdote: *Jesus miraculously multiplied five loaves and two fish to feed 5,000 people.*

Verse: *"Taking the five loaves and the two fish and looking up to heaven, he gave thanks and broke the loaves."* *(Matthew 14:19)*

Riddle: The wind and the waves obeyed me when I told them to be still. Who am I?

Answer: Jesus!

Anecdote: *Jesus calmed a storm while in a boat with His disciples, showing His power over nature.*

Verse: *"He got up, rebuked the wind and said to the waves, 'Quiet! Be still!' Then the wind died down and it was completely calm."* *(Mark 4:39)*

Riddle: I was possessed by many demons, but Jesus set me free. Who am I?
Answer: The man with the legion of demons!

Anecdote: Jesus cast out a legion of demons from a man, freeing him from their control.
Verse: "For Jesus had commanded the impure spirit to come out of the man." (Luke 8:29)

Riddle: I was full of disease, but Jesus touched me, and I became clean. Who am I?
Answer: The leper!

Anecdote: Jesus healed a man with leprosy, restoring him to health.
Verse: "Jesus reached out his hand and touched the man. 'I am willing,' he said. 'Be clean!' Immediately he was cleansed of his leprosy." (Matthew 8:3)

Riddle: I was cursed by Jesus because I had leaves but no fruit. What am I?
Answer: The fig tree!

Anecdote: Jesus cursed a fig tree as a lesson on spiritual fruitfulness after finding no fruit on it.
Verse: "Seeing a fig tree by the road, he went up to it but found nothing on it except leaves. Then he said to it, 'May you never bear fruit again!'" (Matthew 21:19)

CHAPTER THREE

Parables and Teachings

Knock, knock.
Who's there?
Mustard.
Mustard who?
Mustard seed—small but mighty!

Anecdote: Jesus taught that faith as small as a mustard seed can move mountains, illustrating the power of even the smallest amount of true belief.
Verse: "If you have faith as small as a mustard seed, you can say to this mountain, 'Move from here to there,' and it will move." (Matthew 17:20)

Knock, knock.
Who's there?
Sower.
Sower who?
Sower seeds, and you'll reap what you grow!

Anecdote: *In the Parable of the Sower, Jesus explained that seeds (God's word) sown on different types of soil (hearts) produce different results.*
Verse: *"A farmer went out to sow his seed... Some fell on good soil, where it produced a crop." (Matthew 13:3-8)*

Knock, knock.
Who's there?
Shepherd.
Shepherd who?
Shepherd you listen to His voice!

Anecdote: *In the Parable of the Good Shepherd, Jesus describes Himself as the shepherd who cares for His sheep, leading them safely.*
Verse: *"I am the good shepherd. The good shepherd lays down his life for the sheep." (John 10:11)*

Knock, knock.
Who's there?
Prodigal.
Prodigal who?
Prodigal son—coming home for forgiveness!

Anecdote: *The Parable of the Prodigal Son shows God's willingness to forgive and welcome us back, no matter how far we've wandered.*

Verse: *"But while he was still a long way off, his father saw him and was filled with compassion for him." (Luke 15:20)*

Knock, knock.

Who's there?

Wise.

Wise who?

Wise man builds on the rock, not the sand!

Anecdote: *Jesus taught in the Parable of the Wise and Foolish Builders that a foundation built on His teachings is unshakable, like a house built on rock.*

Verse: *"The wise man built his house on the rock. The rain came down, the streams rose, and the winds blew... yet it did not fall." (Matthew 7:24-25)*

Knock, knock.

Who's there?

Lamp.

Lamp who?

Lamp under a basket? Don't hide your light!

Anecdote: *Jesus taught that we shouldn't hide the light of truth and good deeds, but instead, let it shine for all to see.*

Verse: *"Neither do people light a lamp and put it under a bowl. Instead, they put it on its stand, and it gives light to everyone in the house." (Matthew 5:15)*

Knock, knock.
Who's there?
Good.
Good who?
Good Samaritan—here to lend a helping hand!

Anecdote: In the Parable of the Good Samaritan, Jesus teaches the importance of loving your neighbor, regardless of differences or expectations.
Verse: "But a Samaritan... took pity on him... and took care of him." (Luke 10:33-34)

Knock, knock.
Who's there?
Pearl.
Pearl who?
Pearl of great value—worth giving up everything for!

Anecdote: Jesus taught that the Kingdom of Heaven is like a pearl of great price, worth giving up all earthly possessions to obtain.
Verse: "When he found one of great value, he went away and sold everything he had and bought it." (Matthew 13:46)

Knock, knock.
Who's there?
Lost.
Lost who?
Lost sheep—glad the shepherd found me!

Anecdote: In the Parable of the Lost Sheep, Jesus speaks of the shepherd who leaves the 99 sheep to find the one that is lost, showing God's love for each individual.

Verse: *"Suppose one of you has a hundred sheep and loses one... Does he not go after the lost sheep until he finds it?" (Luke 15:4)*

Knock, knock.
Who's there?
Talent.
Talent who?
Talent you should invest and not bury!

Anecdote: *In the Parable of the Talents, Jesus teaches the importance of using the gifts God gives us, rather than hiding them away.*
Verse: *"Well done, good and faithful servant! You have been faithful with a few things; I will put you in charge of many things." (Matthew 25:21)*

Punny Jokes

Joke: Why did the sower start a band?
A: Because he wanted to "rock" the soil!

Anecdote: *In the Parable of the Sower, Jesus explains how seeds (God's word) fall on different types of soil, representing the conditions of people's hearts.*
Verse: *"A farmer went out to sow his seed... Some fell on rocky places, where it did not have much soil." (Matthew 13:3-5)*

Joke: Why did the mustard seed become famous?
A: Because it had "growing" influence!

Anecdote: Jesus compared the Kingdom of Heaven to a mustard seed, showing how something small can grow into something great.
Verse: "Though it is the smallest of all seeds, yet when it grows, it is the largest of garden plants." (Matthew 13:32)

Joke: Why did the wise man bring an umbrella to build his house?
A: Because he wanted to weather the storm!

Anecdote: In the Parable of the Wise and Foolish Builders, Jesus teaches that a strong foundation (built on His teachings) can withstand the storms of life.
Verse: "The rain came down, the streams rose, and the winds blew... yet it did not fall, because it had its foundation on the rock." (Matthew 7:25)

Joke: Why did the lamp break up with the basket?
A: Because it didn't want to be "kept in the dark" anymore!

Anecdote: Jesus teaches that we should not hide our light (good works and truth) but let it shine for others to see.
Verse: "Neither do people light a lamp and put it under a bowl. Instead, they put it on its stand." (Matthew 5:15)

Joke: Why was the Good Samaritan such a good cook?

A: Because he always "spices" up life with kindness!

Anecdote: In the Parable of the Good Samaritan, Jesus emphasizes loving your neighbor through acts of compassion and kindness.
Verse: "But a Samaritan, as he traveled, came where the man was; and when he saw him, he took pity on him." (Luke 10:33)

Joke: Why did the Prodigal Son become a chef?
A: Because he "whipped" up a story about eating with pigs!

Anecdote: In the Parable of the Prodigal Son, a young man squanders his inheritance and finds himself so hungry he considers eating pig food before returning home.
Verse: "He longed to fill his stomach with the pods that the pigs were eating." (Luke 15:16)

Joke: Why did the rich man refuse to sell his field?
A: Because he couldn't "bear" to part with his treasure!

Anecdote: In the Parable of the Hidden Treasure, Jesus teaches that the Kingdom of Heaven is worth more than anything we own.
Verse: "The kingdom of heaven is like treasure hidden in a field. When a man found it, he... sold all he had and bought that field." (Matthew 13:44)

Joke: Why did the foolish virgins fail their class?
A: Because they "burned out" before the exam!

Anecdote: *In the Parable of the Ten Virgins, five wise virgins had enough oil for their lamps, but the foolish ones did not, symbolizing the need to always be prepared.*
Verse: *"The foolish ones said to the wise, 'Give us some of your oil; our lamps are going out.'" (Matthew 25:8)*

Joke: Why did the lost sheep feel bad?
A: Because it knew it had "baaad" judgment!

Anecdote: *Jesus teaches in the Parable of the Lost Sheep that God seeks out every lost individual with great love, no matter how far they have wandered.*
Verse: *"Suppose one of you has a hundred sheep and loses one of them. Doesn't he leave the ninety-nine and go after the lost sheep until he finds it?" (Luke 15:4)*

Joke: Why didn't the Pharisee like Jesus' parables?
A: Because they always "revealed" the truth!

Anecdote: *Jesus often used parables to explain spiritual truths, which the Pharisees sometimes misunderstood or rejected because they were unwilling to see the deeper meaning.*
Verse: *"This is why I speak to them in parables: 'Though seeing, they do not see; though hearing, they do not hear or understand.'" (Matthew 13:13)*

One Liners

Joke: The mustard seed started small, but now it's the king of the garden—talk about a "growing" faith!

Anecdote: *In the Parable of the Mustard Seed, Jesus illustrates that even a small amount of faith can grow into something significant.*
Verse: *"Though it is the smallest of all seeds, yet when it grows, it is the largest of garden plants." (Matthew 13:32)*

Joke: The wise man built his house on the rock—he clearly knew how to "solidify" his foundation!

Anecdote: *The Parable of the Wise and Foolish Builders teaches the importance of a strong foundation based on Jesus' teachings.*
Verse: *"The rain came down, the streams rose, and the winds blew... yet it did not fall, because it had its foundation on the rock." (Matthew 7:25)*

Joke: The sower's secret to success? He knew how to "plant" good news in every heart!

Anecdote: In the Parable of the Sower, Jesus explains that the seeds represent God's word, and the soil types symbolize people's hearts.
Verse: "A farmer went out to sow his seed... Some fell on good soil, where it produced a crop." (Matthew 13:3-8)

Joke: The Good Samaritan didn't just pass by; he made sure to "bandage" the situation!

Anecdote: In the Parable of the Good Samaritan, Jesus teaches about loving your neighbor by showing compassion, even to strangers.
Verse: "He went to him and bandaged his wounds... and took care of him." (Luke 10:34)

Joke: The Prodigal Son came back home because he couldn't handle being "piggy" with his decisions anymore!

Anecdote: The Parable of the Prodigal Son tells of a young man who squandered his inheritance but found forgiveness when he returned home.
Verse: "When he came to his senses, he said... 'I will set out and go back to my father.'" (Luke 15:17-18)

Joke: The lost sheep was baaad at directions, but the shepherd never lost "track"!

Anecdote: In the Parable of the Lost Sheep, Jesus highlights God's love for every individual, even those who have wandered away.
Verse: "Suppose one of you has a hundred sheep and loses one... doesn't he go after the lost sheep until he finds it?" (Luke 15:4)

Joke: The foolish virgins' lamps went out—they just didn't have enough "oil" for the occasion!

Anecdote: In the Parable of the Ten Virgins, Jesus emphasizes being prepared for His return, like the wise virgins who had enough oil for their lamps.
Verse: "The foolish ones said to the wise, 'Give us some of your oil; our lamps are going out.'" (Matthew 25:8)

Joke: The man who found the hidden treasure wasn't greedy; he just knew when to "cash in" on the kingdom!

Anecdote: In the Parable of the Hidden Treasure, Jesus explains that the Kingdom of Heaven is worth more than anything else we could ever own.
Verse: "When a man found it, he hid it again, and then in his joy went and sold all he had and bought that field." (Matthew 13:44)

Joke: The Pharisee who prayed loudly must have had a "holier-than-thou" megaphone!
Anecdote: In the Parable of the Pharisee and the Tax Collector, Jesus warns against self-righteousness and teaches the value of humility before God.
Verse: "For all those who exalt themselves will be humbled, and those who humble themselves will be exalted." (Luke 18:14)

Joke: The wise man knew how to "rock" his foundation—he built it to last through any storm!

Anecdote: *The Parable of the Wise Builder teaches that living by Jesus' words provides a strong foundation to weather life's storms.*
Verse: *"The rain came down, the streams rose, and the winds blew... yet it did not fall." (Matthew 7:25)*

Riddle Jokes

Riddle: I'm small but mighty, I can grow a tree. What am I?
Answer: A mustard seed!
Anecdote: *Jesus compared the Kingdom of Heaven to a mustard seed, illustrating that even the smallest faith can lead to great things.*
Verse: *"Though it is the smallest of all seeds, yet when it grows, it is the largest of garden plants." (Matthew 13:32)*

Riddle: I can be wise or foolish, built on rock or sand. What am I?
Answer: A house!

Anecdote: *The Parable of the Wise and Foolish Builders teaches the importance of a solid foundation based on Jesus' teachings.*
Verse: *"The rain came down, the streams rose, and the winds blew... yet it did not fall, because it had its foundation on the rock." (Matthew 7:25)*

Riddle: I'm sown in different soils, some bear fruit, while others don't. What am I?
Answer: A seed!

Anecdote: *In the Parable of the Sower, Jesus describes how God's word is received differently by people's hearts.*
Verse: *"A farmer went out to sow his seed... Some fell on good soil, where it produced a crop." (Matthew 13:3-8)*

Riddle: I'm the one who stops to help, while others just walk by. Who am I?
Answer: The Good Samaritan!

Anecdote: *Jesus uses the Parable of the Good Samaritan to teach about loving your neighbor and showing compassion.*
Verse: *"He went to him and bandaged his wounds... and took care of him." (Luke 10:34)*

Riddle: I took my inheritance and left home, but came back when I lost it all. Who am I?
Answer: The Prodigal Son!

Anecdote: *The Parable of the Prodigal Son illustrates God's forgiveness and love for those who repent and return to Him.*

Verse: *"When he came to his senses, he said... 'I will set out and go back to my father.'"*
(Luke 15:17-18)

Riddle: I'm a treasure hidden in a field, worth selling everything for. What am I?
Answer: The Kingdom of Heaven!

Anecdote: *In the Parable of the Hidden Treasure, Jesus teaches that the Kingdom of Heaven is of immeasurable value.*
Verse: *"The kingdom of heaven is like treasure hidden in a field." (Matthew 13:44)*

Riddle: I have ten friends, but only five are wise with their oil. Who am I?
Answer: The Ten Virgins!

Anecdote: *In the Parable of the Ten Virgins, Jesus emphasizes the importance of being prepared for His return.*
Verse: *"The foolish ones said to the wise, 'Give us some of your oil; our lamps are going out.'" (Matthew 25:8)*

Riddle: I'm the one who wandered off, but my shepherd came to find me. Who am I?
Answer: The lost sheep!

Anecdote: *The Parable of the Lost Sheep shows God's great love and pursuit of every individual who strays from Him.*
Verse: *"Does he not go after the lost sheep until he finds it?" (Luke 15:4)*

Riddle: I'm the man who prays loudly to be seen, but the tax collector keeps his head down. Who am I?
Answer: The Pharisee!

Anecdote: In the Parable of the Pharisee and the Tax Collector, Jesus teaches about humility and the dangers of self-righteousness.
Verse: "For all those who exalt themselves will be humbled." (Luke 18:14)

Riddle: I'm a field where a man found treasure, but I need to sell all to get it. What am I?
Answer: The field with hidden treasure!

Anecdote: In this parable, Jesus teaches that the Kingdom of Heaven is worth giving up everything we have to attain.
Verse: "When he found it, he hid it again, and then in his joy went and sold all he had and bought that field." (Matthew 13:44)

CHAPTER FOUR

Crucifixion and Resurrection

Knock, knock.
Who's there?
Rolled.
Rolled who?
Rolled the stone away! He is risen!

Anecdote: *When the women arrived at Jesus' tomb, they found that the stone had been rolled away, marking His resurrection.*
Verse: *"They found the stone rolled away from the tomb, but when they entered, they did not find the body of the Lord Jesus." (Luke 24:2-3)*

Knock, knock.

Who's there?
Soldiers.
Soldiers who?
Soldiers couldn't stop Him! He's alive!

Anecdote: Roman soldiers were stationed at Jesus' tomb to guard it, but they could not prevent His resurrection.
Verse: "Take a guard... So they went and made the tomb secure by putting a seal on the stone and posting the guard." (Matthew 27:65-66)

Knock, knock.
Who's there?
Cross.
Cross who?
Cross your heart—Jesus carried it for you!
Anecdote: Jesus bore His own cross to Calvary, symbolizing the weight of humanity's sins that He carried.
Verse: "Carrying his own cross, he went out to the place of the Skull." (John 19:17)

Knock, knock.
Who's there?
Empty.
Empty who?
Empty tomb! Jesus isn't here, He's risen!

Anecdote: The empty tomb symbolizes the victory of Jesus over death, as He was raised from the dead.
Verse: "Why do you look for the living among the dead? He is not here; he has risen!" (Luke 24:5-6)

Knock, knock.

Who's there?

Crown.

Crown who?

Crown of thorns—but He's now crowned King of Kings!

Anecdote: *Jesus wore a crown of thorns during His crucifixion, but His resurrection affirms His eternal reign.*

Verse: *"They twisted together a crown of thorns and set it on his head." (John 19:2)*

Knock, knock.

Who's there?

It is finished.

It is finished who?

Exactly! Jesus said it is finished, and our sins are paid!

Anecdote: *Jesus declared "It is finished" before His death, signifying the completion of His redemptive work.*

Verse: *"When he had received the drink, Jesus said, 'It is finished.'" (John 19:30)*

Knock, knock.

Who's there?

Mary.

Mary who?

Mary Magdalene! First to see the risen Lord!

Anecdote: *Mary Magdalene was the first to witness the resurrected Jesus, becoming the first evangelist of the resurrection.*

Verse: "*Mary Magdalene went to the disciples with the news: 'I have seen the Lord!'*" *(John 20:18)*

Knock, knock.
Who's there?
Veil.
Veil who?
Veil torn! Jesus opened the way to God!

Anecdote: At Jesus' death, the temple veil was torn, symbolizing the opening of direct access to God through Christ.
Verse: "*The curtain of the temple was torn in two from top to bottom.*" *(Mark 15:38)*

Knock, knock.
Who's there?
Grave.
Grave who?
Grave's got no victory—Jesus conquered it!
Anecdote: Jesus' resurrection broke the power of death and the grave, securing eternal life for believers.
Verse: "*Where, O death, is your victory? Where, O death, is your sting?*" *(1 Corinthians 15:55)*

Knock, knock.
Who's there?
Thomas.
Thomas who?

Thomas the doubter—until he saw Jesus alive!

Anecdote: *Thomas, one of Jesus' disciples, doubted the resurrection until he saw Jesus in person and touched His wounds.*
Verse: *"Put your finger here; see my hands... Stop doubting and believe." (John 20:27)*

Punny Jokes

Joke: Why did Jesus' tomb become so popular?
Answer: Because it was a grave success!

Anecdote: *The empty tomb where Jesus was laid became a symbol of victory over death.*
Verse: *"He is not here; he has risen!" (Luke 24:6)*

Joke: What did the Roman soldier say after the tomb was found empty?
Answer: "This is an open-and-shut case!"

Anecdote: *The Roman soldiers guarding the tomb couldn't stop the resurrection.*
Verse: *"The guards were so afraid of him that they shook and became like dead men."*
(Matthew 28:4)

Joke: Why don't we call Jesus' resurrection day "Sad Sunday"?
Answer: Because it's Sonday, and the Son has risen!

Anecdote: *The resurrection of Jesus is celebrated joyfully because He conquered death.*
Verse: *"On the first day of the week, very early in the morning, the women took the spices... and found the stone rolled away." (Luke 24:1-2)*

Joke: Why didn't the disciples need to worry about Jesus after the crucifixion?
Answer: Because He nailed the plan of salvation!

Anecdote: *Jesus' crucifixion was the fulfillment of God's plan to redeem mankind.*
Verse: *"It is finished." (John 19:30)*

Joke: What did the angel say when the women came to Jesus' tomb?
Answer: "He's a-live wire—you can't keep Him in the grave!"

Anecdote: *The angels announced to the women that Jesus had risen from the dead.*
Verse: *"Why do you look for the living among the dead? He is not here; he has risen!" (Luke 24:5-6)*

Joke: Why was the stone rolled away from Jesus' tomb?
Answer: Because He didn't want to rock the boat—He just rose!

Anecdote: *The large stone was rolled away by an angel, marking Jesus' resurrection.*
Verse: *"An angel of the Lord came down from heaven and, going to the tomb, rolled back the stone." (Matthew 28:2)*

Joke: What did Jesus say when He appeared to the disciples after the resurrection?
Answer: "You guys didn't see that coming, did you?"

Anecdote: Jesus appeared to His disciples after His resurrection, surprising them with His presence.
Verse: "Jesus came and stood among them and said, 'Peace be with you!'" (John 20:19)

Joke: Why was the resurrection like a surprise party for the disciples?
Answer: Because they didn't expect Jesus to pop out of the tomb!

Anecdote: Even though Jesus predicted His resurrection, the disciples were initially shocked to find the empty tomb.
Verse: "They still did not understand from Scripture that Jesus had to rise from the dead." (John 20:9)

Joke: Why didn't Jesus need His tomb for long?
Answer: Because He was just borrowing it for the weekend!

Anecdote: Jesus was buried in a tomb, but His resurrection made it only temporary.
Verse: "Joseph of Arimathea... placed it in his own new tomb." (Matthew 27:59-60)

Joke: What did Jesus say after His resurrection when Thomas doubted?
Answer: "Don't be cross with Me, Thomas—here are My hands!"

Anecdote: *Thomas doubted Jesus' resurrection until he saw and touched Jesus' wounds from the crucifixion.*
Verse: *"Put your finger here; see my hands... Stop doubting and believe." (John 20:27)*

One Liner Jokes

Joke: Jesus didn't stay in the tomb because He had bigger plans—like saving the world!
Anecdote: *Jesus' resurrection fulfilled God's ultimate plan for salvation, defeating death.*
Verse: *"He is not here; he has risen, just as he said." (Matthew 28:6)*

Joke: The stone wasn't rolled away to let Jesus out; it was rolled away to let us in!

Anecdote: *The open tomb symbolized the beginning of new life for believers in Christ.*
Verse: *"They found the stone rolled away from the tomb." (Luke 24:2)*

Joke: Jesus' resurrection wasn't a comeback—it was the ultimate victory!

Anecdote: *Jesus' rising from the dead signifies His triumph over sin and death.*

Verse: *"Where, O death, is your victory? Where, O death, is your sting?" (1 Corinthians 15:55)*

Joke: Jesus' grave wasn't the end—it was the start of a new beginning!

Anecdote: The empty tomb is a testament to eternal life through Jesus' sacrifice and resurrection.
Verse: "He is not here; he has risen!" (Luke 24:6)

Joke: When Jesus said, "It is finished," He wasn't talking about His story—He was talking about sin's power!

Anecdote: Jesus' death on the cross completed His mission to pay for humanity's sins.
Verse: "When he had received the drink, Jesus said, 'It is finished.'" (John 19:30)

Joke: The crucifixion wasn't just painful—it was deeply moving because it moved the veil of separation from God!

Anecdote: The temple veil tearing at Jesus' death symbolized the removal of the barrier between God and humanity.
Verse: "The curtain of the temple was torn in two from top to bottom." (Mark 15:38)

Joke: They sealed the tomb, but not even death could lock Jesus in!

Anecdote: The tomb was sealed and guarded, but Jesus rose, showing His power over death.
Verse: "So they went and made the tomb secure by putting a seal on the stone and posting the guard." (Matthew 27:66)

Joke: Jesus didn't rise to make headlines—He rose to change our hearts!

Anecdote: The resurrection isn't just a historical event; it's a transformative moment for believers.
Verse: "If Christ has not been raised, your faith is futile; you are still in your sins." (1 Corinthians 15:17)

Joke: Jesus didn't just conquer death—He gave us eternal life as a free bonus!

Anecdote: Through Jesus' resurrection, believers are promised eternal life with Him.
Verse: "For as in Adam all die, so in Christ all will be made alive." (1 Corinthians 15:22)

Joke: Doubting Thomas should've known—Jesus always delivers on His promises!

Anecdote: After Jesus' resurrection, Thomas initially doubted, but Jesus appeared and showed him His wounds.
Verse: "Because you have seen me, you have believed; blessed are those who have not seen and yet have believed." (John 20:29)

Riddle Jokes

Riddle: What has a crown but doesn't sit on a throne, yet is the King of kings?
Answer: Jesus with the crown of thorns.

Anecdote: Jesus wore a crown of thorns during His crucifixion, a mocking symbol that became a powerful image of His kingship.
Verse: "And then twisted together a crown of thorns and set it on his head." (John 19:2)

Riddle: What was borrowed for three days but never used again?
Answer: Jesus' tomb.

Anecdote: Jesus was placed in a tomb, but He didn't stay there long—He rose after three days.
Verse: "Joseph of Arimathea... placed it in his own new tomb." (Matthew 27:59-60)

Riddle: What was sealed with a stone, guarded by soldiers, but couldn't hold its occupant?
Answer: Jesus' tomb.

Anecdote: Though the tomb was sealed and guarded, it couldn't keep Jesus inside.

Verse: *"The guards were so afraid of him that they shook and became like dead men."* *(Matthew 28:4)*

Riddle: What seemed like the end but turned out to be a new beginning?
Answer: The crucifixion of Jesus.

Anecdote: *Jesus' death on the cross appeared to be the end, but His resurrection signaled a new chapter for humanity.*
Verse: *"It is finished." (John 19:30)*

Riddle: What was rolled away to show that death had lost its grip?
Answer: The stone from Jesus' tomb.

Anecdote: *The stone was rolled away from Jesus' tomb, signifying that death could not hold Him.*
Verse: *"They found the stone rolled away from the tomb." (Luke 24:2)*

Riddle: What was pierced but still healed the world?
Answer: Jesus' hands and side.

Anecdote: *Jesus' hands and side were pierced during the crucifixion, but through His wounds, healing and salvation came.*
Verse: *"But he was pierced for our transgressions." (Isaiah 53:5)*

Riddle: What was meant to mock but ended up proving royal authority?

Answer: The sign that said "King of the Jews" above Jesus' head.

Anecdote: *Pilate placed a sign on the cross that mocked Jesus, yet it declared the truth of His kingship.*
Verse: *"Pilate had a notice prepared and fastened to the cross. It read: JESUS OF NAZARETH, THE KING OF THE JEWS." (John 19:19)*

Riddle: What appeared lifeless on Friday but was full of life by Sunday?
Answer: Jesus' body in the tomb.

Anecdote: *Jesus' crucified body lay in the tomb for three days before His resurrection on Sunday morning.*
Verse: *"On the first day of the week... they found the stone rolled away from the tomb."* (Luke 24:1-2)

Riddle: What could not be conquered by nails, wood, or a crown of thorns?
Answer: Jesus' love for humanity.

Anecdote: *Jesus' love and sacrifice on the cross demonstrated His unstoppable love for all mankind.*
Verse: *"Greater love has no one than this: to lay down one's life for one's friends." (John 15:13)*

Riddle: What was dead for three days but came back more powerful than ever?
Answer: Jesus Christ.

Anecdote: *Jesus' death and resurrection show His power over death and His divine nature.*

Verse: *"I am the resurrection and the life. The one who believes in me will live, even though they die." (John 11:25)*

PART TWO

JESUS' CHARACTER

CHAPTER FIVE

Love and kindness

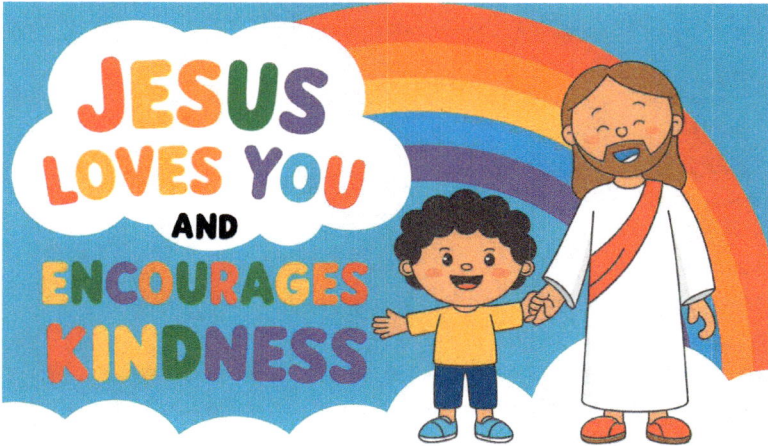

Knock knock.
Who's there?
Jesus.
Jesus who?
Jesus, who laid down His life for you out of love!

Anecdote: Jesus' love was so great that He sacrificed His life to save humanity.
Verse: "Greater love has no one than this: to lay down one's life for one's friends." (John 15:13)

Knock knock.
Who's there?

Grace.

Grace who?

Grace given through the love of Jesus!

Anecdote: Through Jesus' love, grace is freely given to all who believe in Him.
Verse: "For it is by grace you have been saved, through faith." (Ephesians 2:8)

Knock knock.

Who's there?

Mercy.

Mercy who?

Mercy, because Jesus loves you too much to let you go!

Anecdote: Jesus' kindness and mercy bring forgiveness to those who seek Him.
Verse: "But because of his great love for us, God, who is rich in mercy, made us alive with Christ." (Ephesians 2:4-5)

Knock knock.

Who's there?

Peace.

Peace who?

Peace that only comes from Jesus' love!

Anecdote: Jesus offers peace that surpasses all understanding through His love.
Verse: "Peace I leave with you; my peace I give you. I do not give to you as the world gives." (John 14:27)

Knock knock.

Who's there?

Compassion.

Compassion who?

Compassion, like Jesus showing love to the broken-hearted!

Anecdote: Jesus constantly showed compassion and kindness, especially to the downtrodden.

Verse: "When Jesus landed and saw a large crowd, he had compassion on them."
(Matthew 14:14)

Knock knock.

Who's there?

Forgiveness.

Forgiveness who?

Forgiveness, because Jesus' love keeps no record of wrongs!

Anecdote: Jesus' love includes the incredible gift of forgiveness for our sins.

Verse: "If we confess our sins, he is faithful and just and will forgive us our sins." (1 John 1:9)

Knock knock.

Who's there?

Kindness.

Kindness who?

Kindness like Jesus washing His disciples' feet!

Anecdote: Jesus demonstrated humility and kindness when He washed His disciples' feet, an act of love and service.

Verse: *"Now that I, your Lord and Teacher, have washed your feet, you also should wash one another's feet." (John 13:14)*

Knock knock.
Who's there?
Shepherd.
Shepherd who?
The Good Shepherd who loves and cares for His flock!

Anecdote: Jesus called Himself the Good Shepherd, demonstrating His loving care for His followers.
Verse: *"I am the good shepherd. The good shepherd lays down his life for the sheep." (John 10:11)*

Knock knock.
Who's there?
Servant.
Servant who?
The Servant King who loves us by serving us!

Anecdote: *Though He is the King of kings, Jesus came not to be served, but to serve, out of His deep love.*
Verse: *"The Son of Man did not come to be served, but to serve." (Matthew 20:28)*

Knock knock.
Who's there?
Everlasting.

Everlasting who?
Everlasting love, just like Jesus!

Anecdote: Jesus' love is eternal and unchanging, showing His unwavering kindness to all.
Verse: "I have loved you with an everlasting love." (Jeremiah 31:3)

Punny Jokes

Pun: Why did Jesus never lose at hide and seek? Because His love always found you!

Anecdote: Jesus' love is unrelenting and seeks to find and save the lost.
Verse: "For the Son of Man came to seek and to save the lost." (Luke 19:10)

Pun: Jesus is the bread of life, so you know His love is never stale!

Anecdote: Jesus referred to Himself as the bread of life, nourishing souls with His eternal love.
Verse: "I am the bread of life. Whoever comes to me will never go hungry." (John 6:35)

Pun: Jesus' love is like Wi-Fi: it's everywhere, and all you have to do is connect!

Anecdote: *Jesus' love is ever-present and accessible to everyone who seeks Him.*
Verse: *"And surely I am with you always, to the very end of the age." (Matthew 28:20)*

Pun: Jesus' love is so powerful, it can turn a stony heart into a cornerstone!

Anecdote: *Jesus' love transforms hearts and builds people into living stones of faith.*
Verse: *"The stone the builders rejected has become the cornerstone." (Psalm 118:22)*

Pun: Why doesn't Jesus need a GPS? Because His love always leads you home!
Anecdote: *Jesus is the way, the truth, and the life—His love guides us to the Father.*
Verse: *"I am the way and the truth and the life. No one comes to the Father except through me." (John 14:6)*

Pun: Jesus' love is like a good pair of sandals—it supports you every step of the way!

Anecdote: *Jesus' love guides, supports, and strengthens us throughout our journey in life.*
Verse: *"Your word is a lamp for my feet, a light on my path." (Psalm 119:105)*

Pun: Why was Jesus so good at math? Because His love multiplies!

Anecdote: *Jesus' love overflows and multiplies, reaching all who seek Him.*

Verse: *"And may the Lord make your love increase and overflow for each other and for everyone else." (1 Thessalonians 3:12)*

Pun: Jesus' love is like a net—He catches everyone who's falling!

Anecdote: *Jesus called His disciples to be fishers of men, catching souls with the love of God.*
Verse: *"Come, follow me, and I will send you out to fish for people." (Matthew 4:19)*

Pun: Jesus' love is like a sunrise—it's impossible to miss and brightens every day!

Anecdote: *Jesus is the light of the world, and His love shines in the darkness, giving hope and joy.*
Verse: *"I am the light of the world. Whoever follows me will never walk in darkness, but will have the light of life." (John 8:12)*

Pun: Jesus' love is like a hug—you can feel it even when you can't see it!

Anecdote: *Though we may not physically see Jesus, His love surrounds and comforts us at all times.*
Verse: *"Though you have not seen him, you love him; and even though you do not see him now, you believe in him and are filled with an inexpressible and glorious joy." (1 Peter 1:8)*

Joke: Jesus had a knack for loving everyone—even the tax collectors and sinners—talk about a diverse portfolio!

Anecdote: *Jesus welcomed those who were often shunned by society, showing that His love knows no bounds.*
Verse: *"For the Son of Man came to seek and to save the lost." (Luke 19:10)*

Joke: Jesus loved to serve, but He didn't need a waiter's tip—just a thankful heart!

Anecdote: *He demonstrated love through acts of service, like washing His disciples' feet.*
Verse: *"Now that I, your Lord and Teacher, have washed your feet, you also should wash one another's feet." (John 13:14)*

Joke: Jesus' love is like a Wi-Fi signal—strong and available, but you've got to connect!

Anecdote: *His love is always present, waiting for us to reach out and embrace it.*
Verse: *"And surely I am with you always, to the very end of the age." (Matthew 28:20)*

Joke: Jesus taught us to love our neighbors, but let's be honest—some of them make it a real challenge!

Anecdote: *He emphasized love for everyone, even those hard to love.*

Verse: *"Love your neighbor as yourself." (Mark 12:31)*

Joke: Jesus was the original "no judgment" zone—just love and compassion all around!

Anecdote: *He always showed kindness and understanding, even to those who made mistakes.*
Verse: *"He who is without sin among you, let him be the first to throw a stone." (John 8:7)*

Joke: If you think love is patient, just ask Jesus about waiting for us to get it right!

Anecdote: *His patience with humanity is a testament to His unconditional love.*
Verse: *"The Lord is not slow in keeping his promise, as some understand slowness. Instead he is patient with you." (2 Peter 3:9)*

Joke: Jesus didn't just preach love—He practiced it like a pro, and we're all His fans!

Anecdote: *His actions matched His words, exemplifying love in every situation.*

Verse: *"Dear children, let us not love with words or speech but with actions and in truth." (1 John 3:18)*

Joke: Jesus showed us that kindness can be contagious—just look at how it spread among His followers!

Anecdote: *His teachings on love inspired many to act kindly toward others.*
Verse: *"By this everyone will know that you are my disciples, if you love one another." (John 13:35)*

Joke: Jesus didn't have a resume for love—His entire life was one big reference!

Anecdote: *Every moment of His life was an example of love in action.*
Verse: *"But God demonstrates his own love for us in this: While we were still sinners, Christ died for us." (Romans 5:8)*

Joke: Jesus' love is like a good cup of coffee—it's best when it's strong and shared with friends!

Anecdote: *He encourages us to share His love with those around us.*
Verse: *"Let us consider how we may spur one another on toward love and good deeds." (Hebrews 10:24)*

Riddle Jokes

Riddle: What do you call it when Jesus shows His love to everyone, even the least expected?
Answer: A divine surprise!

Anecdote: Jesus often reached out to the marginalized and sinners, demonstrating His inclusive love.
Verse: "For the Son of Man came to seek and to save the lost." (Luke 19:10)

Riddle: What spreads faster than gossip and is more uplifting than a compliment?
Answer: Jesus' love!

Anecdote: His love inspires people to act kindly, creating a ripple effect in communities.
Verse: "By this everyone will know that you are my disciples, if you love one another." (John 13:35)

Riddle: What kind of love can turn enemies into friends and heal the brokenhearted?
Answer: Jesus' love!

Anecdote: His love transformed relationships and offered healing to those in need.

Verse: "He heals the brokenhearted and binds up their wounds." (Psalm 147:3)

Riddle: What is the one thing Jesus shared without limit, and it makes the world brighter?
Answer: His kindness!

Anecdote: Jesus showed kindness to everyone, often surprising them with His compassion.
Verse: "Be kind and compassionate to one another, forgiving each other, just as in Christ God forgave you." (Ephesians 4:32)

Riddle: What did Jesus give freely to the world, and it cost Him everything?
Answer: His love!

Anecdote: Jesus demonstrated sacrificial love by laying down His life for humanity.
Verse: "Greater love has no one than this: to lay down one's life for one's friends." (John 15:13)

Riddle: What can calm storms, heal the sick, and feed the hungry, all while sharing love?
Answer: Jesus' miracles!

Anecdote: His miracles were expressions of His love and care for people in need.
Verse: "Jesus went through all the towns and villages, teaching in their synagogues, proclaiming the good news of the kingdom and healing every disease and sickness." (Matthew 9:35)

Riddle: What is a treasure that grows when shared, yet remains unspent?
Answer: Love!

Anecdote: Jesus taught that love multiplies when given away, enriching both the giver and receiver.
Verse: "And may the Lord make your love increase and overflow for each other and for everyone else." (1 Thessalonians 3:12)

Riddle: What is so powerful that it can change hearts and mend relationships, yet is gentle enough to be whispered?
Answer: Jesus' love!

Anecdote: His love softens hearts and promotes reconciliation.
Verse: "But God demonstrates his own love for us in this: While we were still sinners, Christ died for us." (Romans 5:8)

Riddle: What connects people and brings them together, no matter their differences?
Answer: Love!

Anecdote: Jesus encouraged unity and love among His followers, transcending barriers.
Verse: "Love your neighbor as yourself." (Mark 12:31)

Riddle: What did Jesus say is the greatest commandment that covers all the rest?
Answer: Love!

Anecdote: *Jesus summarized the law with love, emphasizing its importance in our lives.*

Verse: *"Love the Lord your God with all your heart and with all your soul and with all your mind." (Matthew 22:37)*

CHAPTER SIX

Forgiveness and mercy

Knock, knock.
Who's there?
Mercy.
Mercy who?
Mercy me, Jesus forgave me again!

Anecdote: *Jesus' mercy is boundless—He offers forgiveness even when we repeatedly fall.*
Verse: *"Then Peter came to Jesus and asked, 'Lord, how many times shall I forgive my brother or sister who sins against me? Up to seven times?' Jesus answered, 'I tell you, not seven times, but seventy-seven times.'" (Matthew 18:21-22)*

Knock, knock.
Who's there?
Grace.
Grace who?
Grace you didn't deserve, but Jesus gave it anyway!

Anecdote: *Jesus' mercy extends grace to us, even when we are undeserving.*
Verse: *"For it is by grace you have been saved, through faith—and this is not from yourselves, it is the gift of God." (Ephesians 2:8)*

Knock, knock.
Who's there?
Pardon.
Pardon who?
Pardon the interruption, but Jesus forgave your sins!

Anecdote: *Jesus pardoned the sins of many, showing mercy to those who sought Him.*
Verse: *"When Jesus saw their faith, he said to the paralyzed man, 'Son, your sins are forgiven.'" (Mark 2:5)*

Knock, knock.
Who's there?
Forgive.
Forgive who?
Forgive others, just like Jesus forgave you!

Anecdote: *Jesus taught that just as we receive mercy, we should extend it to others.*
Verse: *"And forgive us our debts, as we also have forgiven our debtors." (Matthew 6:12)*

Knock, knock.
Who's there?
Second.
Second who?
Second chances are Jesus' specialty!

Anecdote: Jesus gave many people a second chance, including Peter after he denied Him three times.
Verse: "The Lord turned and looked straight at Peter. Then Peter remembered the word the Lord had spoken to him." (Luke 22:61)

Knock, knock.
Who's there?
Peace.
Peace who?
Peace be with you, Jesus forgave your sins!

Anecdote: After His resurrection, Jesus brought peace to His disciples, forgiving them despite their fear and doubt.
Verse: "Peace be with you! As the Father has sent me, I am sending you." (John 20:21)

Knock, knock.
Who's there?
Repent.
Repent who?
Repent, and Jesus will always forgive you!

Anecdote: Jesus emphasized the importance of repentance, assuring that forgiveness follows genuine repentance.
Verse: "If we confess our sins, he is faithful and just and will forgive us our sins and purify us from all unrighteousness." (1 John 1:9)

Knock, knock.
Who's there?
Prodigal.
Prodigal who?
Prodigal son returned, and Jesus threw a party!

Anecdote: Jesus' parable of the Prodigal Son shows God's incredible mercy and willingness to forgive when we return to Him.
Verse: "But while he was still a long way off, his father saw him and was filled with compassion for him." (Luke 15:20)

Knock, knock.
Who's there?
Lost.
Lost who?
Lost sheep found, thanks to Jesus' mercy!

Anecdote: Jesus shared the parable of the lost sheep to illustrate how He seeks out and forgives those who stray.
Verse: "I tell you that in the same way there will be more rejoicing in heaven over one sinner who repents." (Luke 15:7)

Knock, knock.

Who's there?

Cross.

Cross who?

Cross out your sins, Jesus already took them to the cross!

Anecdote: *Jesus showed the ultimate act of mercy by dying on the cross for the forgiveness of sins.*

Verse: *"He himself bore our sins in his body on the cross, so that we might die to sins and live for righteousness." (1 Peter 2:24)*

Punny Jokes

Joke: Jesus doesn't hold a grudge—He nailed it to the cross instead!

Anecdote: *Jesus' ultimate act of forgiveness was His sacrifice on the cross for the sins of humanity.*

Verse: *"He canceled the record of the charges against us and took it away by nailing it to the cross." (Colossians 2:14)*

Joke: Why didn't Jesus ever get angry about betrayal? Because He knew how to forgive and let Judas go!

Anecdote: *Even after Judas betrayed Jesus, Jesus showed mercy in how He handled the situation.*
Verse: *"Friend, do what you came for." (Matthew 26:50)*

Joke: Jesus' mercy is like Wi-Fi—always available but you need to connect to it!

Anecdote: *Jesus' forgiveness is always offered to those who seek it through faith.*
Verse: *"If we confess our sins, he is faithful and just to forgive us our sins and to cleanse us from all unrighteousness." (1 John 1:9)*

Joke: Why is Jesus the best at forgiving? Because He knows how to cross out your mistakes!

Anecdote: *Jesus' death on the cross symbolizes the cancellation of all sins for those who believe.*
Verse: *"It is finished." (John 19:30)*

Joke: Jesus doesn't give you the silent treatment when you mess up—He gives you a second chance!

Anecdote: *Peter denied Jesus three times, yet Jesus restored him with forgiveness and love.*
Verse: *"Jesus said to him, 'Feed my sheep.'" (John 21:17)*

Joke: Why doesn't Jesus mind if you're a mess? Because He's the King of clean slates!

Anecdote: *Jesus wipes away the stains of sin with His mercy, giving everyone a fresh start.*
Verse: *"Though your sins are like scarlet, they shall be as white as snow." (Isaiah 1:18)*

Joke: Jesus doesn't carry grudges—He carries the cross instead!

Anecdote: *Jesus bore the weight of our sins on the cross, freeing us from guilt and shame.*
Verse: *"Surely he took up our pain and bore our suffering." (Isaiah 53:4)*

Joke: Why did Jesus love teaching forgiveness? Because He was all about lesson learned, not mistake earned!

Anecdote: *Jesus emphasized forgiveness as a way of learning from mistakes, not being defined by them.*
Verse: *"Forgive us our debts, as we also have forgiven our debtors." (Matthew 6:12)*

Joke: Why did Jesus forgive so easily? Because He knew that love covers a multitude of sins!

Anecdote: *Jesus' love is what enables Him to show mercy and forgiveness to even the greatest of sinners.*

Verse: *"Above all, love each other deeply, because love covers over a multitude of sins." (1 Peter 4:8)*

Joke: Jesus didn't believe in casting stones—He believed in casting forgiveness!

Anecdote: *When others wanted to stone the woman caught in adultery, Jesus offered her mercy instead.*
Verse: *"Let any one of you who is without sin be the first to throw a stone at her." (John 8:7)*

One Liner Jokes

Joke: Jesus doesn't just forgive once—He's in the business of unlimited forgiveness!

Anecdote: *Jesus taught Peter that we should forgive "seventy-seven times," meaning forgiveness has no limit.*
Verse: *"I tell you, not seven times, but seventy-seven times." (Matthew 18:22)*

Joke: When Jesus forgives, He doesn't keep a receipt—He wipes the slate completely clean!

Anecdote: *Jesus' forgiveness erases our sins, rather than holding them against us.*

Verse: *"As far as the east is from the west, so far has he removed our transgressions from us." (Psalm 103:12)*

Joke: Jesus forgives faster than you can say, "I'm sorry"—He's always ready to redeem!

Anecdote: *Jesus offered immediate forgiveness to the repentant criminal on the cross.*
Verse: *"Truly I tell you, today you will be with me in paradise." (Luke 23:43)*

Joke: Jesus never asks, "Are you sure you're sorry?"—He just says, "You're forgiven."

Anecdote: *Jesus forgave the woman caught in adultery without question, simply telling her to sin no more.*
Verse: *"Neither do I condemn you. Go now and leave your life of sin." (John 8:11)*

Joke: Jesus doesn't do grudges—He does grace!

Anecdote: *Jesus' grace is freely given, even to those who least deserve it, like Saul who persecuted Christians.*
Verse: *"For I will forgive their wickedness and will remember their sins no more." (Hebrews 8:12)*

Joke: Jesus' forgiveness isn't a reward—it's a gift of grace!

Anecdote: The Prodigal Son was welcomed back not because he earned it, but because of his father's mercy.
Verse: "But while he was still a long way off, his father saw him and was filled with compassion." (Luke 15:20)

Joke: Jesus' idea of a second chance? Seventy-seven chances!

Anecdote: Jesus' teaching of limitless forgiveness shows the extent of His mercy.
Verse: "Then Peter came to Jesus and asked...'How many times shall I forgive?'" (Matthew 18:21-22)

Joke: With Jesus, no sin is too big to be forgiven—He's already paid the price!

Anecdote: Jesus' sacrifice on the cross was for all sins, no matter how great or small.
Verse: "He is the atoning sacrifice for our sins, and not only for ours but also for the sins of the whole world." (1 John 2:2)

Joke: Jesus forgives so quickly, He makes it look like sin never even happened!

Anecdote: Jesus restores us fully, washing away all our guilt and shame.
Verse: "Though your sins are like scarlet, they shall be as white as snow." (Isaiah 1:18)

Joke: Jesus doesn't write people off—He rewrites their story of redemption!
Anecdote: Jesus turned Paul, a persecutor of Christians, into one of the greatest apostles.

Verse: *"But for that very reason I was shown mercy so that in me...Christ Jesus might display his immense patience." (1 Timothy 1:16)*

Riddle Jokes

Riddle: What's something you can never out-sin, no matter how hard you try?
Answer: Jesus' mercy.

Anecdote: Jesus' mercy is boundless, forgiving even the most grievous of sins.
Verse: "But where sin increased, grace increased all the more." (Romans 5:20)

Riddle: What's invisible, but removes all your mistakes?
Answer: Jesus' forgiveness.

Anecdote: His forgiveness is unseen, but it wipes our record clean.
Verse: "I will forgive their wickedness and will remember their sins no more." (Jeremiah 31:34)

Riddle: What has no limits, doesn't keep score, and is offered 77 times?
Answer: Jesus' forgiveness.

Anecdote: Jesus teaches unlimited forgiveness, way beyond human counting.
Verse: "I tell you, not seven times, but seventy-seven times." (Matthew 18:22)

Riddle: What cancels debts but never expects repayment?
Answer: Jesus' forgiveness and grace.

Anecdote: *Jesus' sacrifice on the cross paid for our sins, asking only for faith in return.*
Verse: *"Having canceled the charge of our legal indebtedness...he has taken it away, nailing it to the cross." (Colossians 2:14)*

Riddle: What covers everything but doesn't weigh you down?
Answer: Jesus' mercy.

Anecdote: *Jesus' mercy covers all sins, lifting burdens instead of adding them.*
Verse: *"Come to me, all you who are weary and burdened, and I will give you rest." (Matthew 11:28)*

Riddle: What did Jesus offer that nobody asked for but everyone needed?
Answer: Forgiveness on the cross.

Anecdote: *Jesus' sacrifice was for all, even those who didn't recognize their need for it.*
Verse: *"Father, forgive them, for they do not know what they are doing." (Luke 23:34)*

Riddle: What makes the most stubborn of hearts soft and the most guilty feel clean?
Answer: Jesus' forgiveness.

Anecdote: *His mercy changes lives, transforming hearts from hard to humble.*
Verse: *"I will give you a new heart and put a new spirit in you; I will remove from you your heart of stone." (Ezekiel 36:26)*

Riddle: What can wipe away sins but never leaves a trace?
Answer: Jesus' forgiveness.

Anecdote: His forgiveness completely erases our past wrongs.
Verse: "As far as the east is from the west, so far has he removed our transgressions from us." (Psalm 103:12)

Riddle: What is stronger than judgment and always wins?
Answer: Jesus' mercy.

Anecdote: Mercy triumphs over judgment when Jesus forgives and redeems.
Verse: "Mercy triumphs over judgment." (James 2:13)

Riddle: What turns enemies into friends and sinners into saints?
Answer: Jesus' forgiveness and love.

Anecdote: Saul was transformed from persecutor to apostle through Jesus' mercy.
Verse: "I was shown mercy...so that in me...Christ Jesus might display his immense patience." (1 Timothy 1:16)

CHAPTER SEVEN

Patience and Understanding

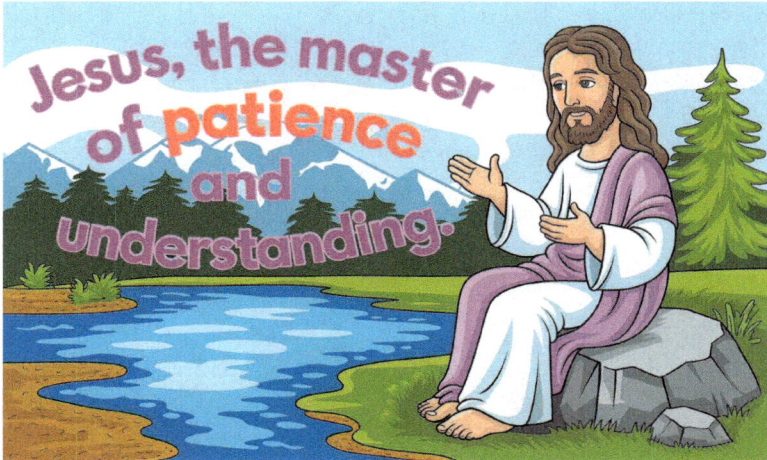

Knock, knock.
Who's there?
Jesus.
Jesus who?
Jesus, still waiting while you figure it out!

Anecdote: *Jesus patiently waits for us to open the door to Him, no matter how long we take.*
Verse: *"Here I am! I stand at the door and knock. If anyone hears my voice and opens the door, I will come in and eat with that person, and they with me." (Revelation 3:20)*

Knock, knock.
Who's there?
Grace.
Grace who?
Grace that waits patiently for you!

Anecdote: Jesus' grace is offered with patience, giving us time to accept His love.
Verse: "The Lord is not slow in keeping his promise...Instead he is patient with you, not wanting anyone to perish." (2 Peter 3:9)

Knock, knock.
Who's there?
Patient.
Patient who?
Patient like Jesus, waiting on your answer!

Anecdote: Jesus shows patience like no one else, waiting for us to come to Him with understanding.
Verse: "The Lord is compassionate and gracious, slow to anger, abounding in love." (Psalm 103:8)

Knock, knock.
Who's there?
Long-suffering.
Long-suffering who?
Long-suffering like Jesus, waiting for you to trust Him!

Anecdote: Jesus is long-suffering, showing understanding even when we falter.

Verse: *"But for that very reason I was shown mercy so that in me, the worst of sinners, Christ Jesus might display his immense patience." (1 Timothy 1:16)*

Knock, knock.
Who's there?
Still here.
Still here who?
Still here, just like Jesus waiting for you to come around!

Anecdote: *Jesus remains with us, patiently waiting for us to turn to Him, no matter how long it takes.*
Verse: *"I will never leave you nor forsake you." (Hebrews 13:5)*

Knock, knock.
Who's there?
Understanding.
Understanding who?
Understanding like Jesus, even when you fall short!

Anecdote: *Jesus understands our weaknesses and still offers His love and grace.*
Verse: *"For we do not have a high priest who is unable to empathize with our weaknesses." (Hebrews 4:15)*

Knock, knock.
Who's there?
Mercy.
Mercy who?

Mercy that waits patiently for you, just like Jesus.

Anecdote: Jesus shows endless mercy, understanding our struggles and waiting for our repentance.
Verse: "His mercies never come to an end; they are new every morning." (Lamentations 3:22-23)

Knock, knock.
Who's there?
Forgive.
Forgive who?
Forgive again, like Jesus!

Anecdote: Jesus doesn't just forgive once, but shows understanding and forgives again and again.
Verse: "Then Peter came to Jesus and asked, 'Lord, how many times shall I forgive...?' Jesus answered, 'I tell you, not seven times, but seventy-seven times.'" (Matthew 18:21-22)

Knock, knock.
Who's there?
Peace.
Peace who?
Peace that waits for you patiently, just like Jesus.

Anecdote: Jesus offers peace to those who seek Him, even when we take our time.
Verse: "Peace I leave with you; my peace I give you... Do not let your hearts be troubled and do not be afraid." (John 14:27)

Knock, knock.
Who's there?
Loving-kindness.
Loving-kindness who?
Loving-kindness, waiting like Jesus does for you!

Anecdote: Jesus' kindness is patient and understanding, always waiting for us to draw near.
Verse: "I have loved you with an everlasting love; I have drawn you with unfailing kindness." (Jeremiah 31:3)

Punny Jokes

Why didn't Jesus rush to Lazarus' side?
Because good things come to those who "wait" four days!

Anecdote: Jesus waited before raising Lazarus to show God's power and glory in patience.
Verse: "So when he heard that Lazarus was sick, he stayed where he was two more days." (John 11:6)

Why does Jesus always have time for us?
Because His schedule is full of patience, not impatience!

Anecdote: *Jesus consistently showed patience with His disciples, even when they didn't understand His teachings.*
Verse: *"How long shall I stay with you? How long shall I put up with you?" (Matthew 17:17)*

How does Jesus wait when we mess up?
With grace and patience—He never "crosses" us out!

Anecdote: *Jesus never gives up on us, showing infinite grace and understanding when we falter.*
Verse: *"The Lord is merciful and gracious, slow to anger and abounding in steadfast love." (Psalm 103:8)*

Why didn't Jesus get upset when the disciples fell asleep in Gethsemane?
Because He knew it's hard to stay "awake" in prayer sometimes!

Anecdote: *Even when His closest friends failed Him in His hour of need, Jesus showed patience.*
Verse: *"Couldn't you men keep watch with me for one hour?" (Matthew 26:40)*

What do you call Jesus' reaction when Peter denied Him three times?
A masterclass in "forgive and forgetfulness"!

Anecdote: *Despite Peter's denial, Jesus forgave him and patiently restored him after the resurrection.*

Verse: *"And the Lord turned and looked at Peter... and Peter wept bitterly." (Luke 22:61-62)*

Why does Jesus never get frustrated when we ask Him the same questions over and over?
Because His love is on "repeat," not retreat!

Anecdote: *Jesus patiently taught His followers, even when they struggled to understand His parables and lessons.*
Verse: *"But the Counselor, the Holy Spirit... will teach you all things and will remind you of everything I have said to you." (John 14:26)*

What did Jesus say when the crowd kept misunderstanding His parables?
"No need to worry—I'm planting seeds of understanding!"

Anecdote: *Jesus knew that even if people didn't understand His teachings immediately, they would grow in their hearts over time.*
Verse: *"But the seed on good soil stands for those with a noble and good heart." (Luke 8:15)*

Why does Jesus never lose His patience when we stray?
Because He's the "Lamb" that leads us back with love!

Anecdote: *Jesus told the parable of the lost sheep, showing His patient care for those who stray from the path.*
Verse: *"Suppose one of you has a hundred sheep and loses one of them. Doesn't he leave the ninety-nine... and go after the lost sheep?" (Luke 15:4)*

How did Jesus respond when Thomas doubted His resurrection?
With a "nail"-biting display of patience!

Anecdote: *Even when Thomas doubted, Jesus gently showed him His wounds, understanding Thomas' need for proof.*
Verse: *"Put your finger here; see my hands. Reach out your hand and put it into my side." (John 20:27)*

Why did Jesus never rush His disciples' faith journey?
Because He believed in slow and "steadfast" growth!

Anecdote: *Jesus nurtured His disciples' faith step by step, knowing growth takes time.*
Verse: *"Let perseverance finish its work so that you may be mature and complete." (James 1:4)*

One Liner Jokes

Jesus waited 40 days in the desert and didn't even complain about the WiFi!

Anecdote: *Jesus fasted for 40 days in the wilderness, showing His patience and reliance on God.*
Verse: *"After fasting forty days and forty nights, he was hungry." (Matthew 4:2)*

Jesus doesn't hit "unfollow" when we mess up—He patiently guides us back!

Anecdote: *The parable of the lost sheep shows how Jesus patiently seeks and restores those who stray.*
Verse: *"And when he finds it, he joyfully puts it on his shoulders." (Luke 15:5)*

Jesus never rushes your prayers; He's got infinite patience on His calendar!

Anecdote: *Jesus always takes the time to hear prayers, never showing impatience.*
Verse: *"Ask and it will be given to you; seek and you will find." (Matthew 7:7)*

Jesus handled Peter's denials with more patience than a saint—literally!

Anecdote: *Jesus showed incredible patience after Peter denied Him three times, restoring him after His resurrection.*
Verse: *"Simon, son of John, do you love me?" (John 21:17)*

Jesus never says "I told you so," even when we keep making the same mistakes!

Anecdote: *Jesus patiently forgave the disciples and others who misunderstood or doubted Him.*

Verse: *"Father, forgive them, for they do not know what they are doing." (Luke 23:34)*

When the disciples argued, Jesus didn't yell; He just gave them a lesson in humility!

Anecdote: *Jesus corrected His disciples with patience when they argued about who was the greatest.*
Verse: *"Anyone who wants to be first must be the very last, and the servant of all." (Mark 9:35)*

Jesus didn't mind waiting for His disciples to understand—He knew some lessons take time!

Anecdote: *Jesus often explained His parables multiple times to help His followers understand.*
Verse: *"The knowledge of the secrets of the kingdom of heaven has been given to you." (Matthew 13:11)*

Jesus didn't rush to heal Lazarus—He was showing patience that even death couldn't defeat!

Anecdote: *Jesus waited before raising Lazarus to demonstrate God's power in perfect timing.*
Verse: *"This sickness will not end in death." (John 11:4)*

Jesus didn't give up on Thomas; He patiently proved that doubts aren't stronger than faith!

Anecdote: *When Thomas doubted Jesus' resurrection, Jesus patiently showed him His wounds.*
Verse: *"Stop doubting and believe." (John 20:27)*

Jesus always sees the big picture—He's never in a rush, and He knows everything works out in time!

Anecdote: *Jesus spoke about the slow, steady growth of God's kingdom, like a mustard seed.*
Verse: *"Though it is the smallest of all seeds, yet when it grows, it is the largest of garden plants." (Matthew 13:32)*

Riddle Jokes

Riddle: I wait in the wilderness for 40 days, resisting temptation without complaint. Who am I?
Answer: Jesus!

Anecdote: *Jesus fasted for 40 days in the desert, demonstrating incredible patience and trust in God.*
Verse: *"After fasting forty days and forty nights, he was hungry." (Matthew 4:2)*

Riddle: I forgive 70 times 7 and never lose patience. Who am I?
Answer: Jesus!

Anecdote: Jesus taught us to forgive endlessly, showing His patience and understanding of human shortcomings.
Verse: "I tell you, not seven times, but seventy-seven times." (Matthew 18:22)

Riddle: I wait outside a tomb for four days, knowing time won't stop me from bringing life back. Who am I?
Answer: Jesus!

Anecdote: Jesus patiently waited before raising Lazarus from the dead, showing God's perfect timing.
Verse: "Lazarus, come out!" (John 11:43)

Riddle: I calm storms, heal the sick, and wait for you to understand—no rush. Who am I?
Answer: Jesus!

Anecdote: Jesus calmed the storm when His disciples panicked, showing patience in teaching them about faith.
Verse: "You of little faith, why are you so afraid?" (Matthew 8:26)

Riddle: I don't scold you for doubt but invite you to touch and see for yourself. Who am I?
Answer: Jesus!

Anecdote: *Jesus showed patience with Thomas, allowing him to touch His wounds after the resurrection.*

Verse: *"Put your finger here; see my hands." (John 20:27)*

Riddle: I sit and teach all day, even when the crowds grow and the questions never end. Who am I?

Answer: Jesus!

Anecdote: *Jesus patiently taught large crowds and answered questions, showing His understanding of their needs.*

Verse: *"He taught them many things by parables." (Mark 4:2)*

Riddle: I heal ten, but only one comes back to thank Me, and I don't lose patience. Who am I?

Answer: Jesus!

Anecdote: *Jesus healed ten lepers but only one returned to thank Him, yet He didn't lose His patience.*

Verse: *"Where are the other nine?" (Luke 17:17)*

Riddle: I see a crowd hungry for both food and understanding, and I give them bread and patience. Who am I?

Answer: Jesus!

Anecdote: *Jesus patiently taught and then miraculously fed 5,000 people with just five loaves and two fish.*

Verse: *"They all ate and were satisfied." (Matthew 14:20)*

Riddle: I let children come to Me, patiently answering their innocent questions and teaching without haste. Who am I?
Answer: Jesus!

Anecdote: Jesus showed patience and love by welcoming children and teaching them about God's kingdom.
Verse: "Let the little children come to me." (Matthew 19:14)

Riddle: I watch you misunderstand My parables but keep explaining with love and patience. Who am I?
Answer: Jesus!

Anecdote: Jesus often had to explain His parables to the disciples, showing patience as they learned.
Verse: "The secret of the kingdom of God has been given to you." (Mark 4:11)

CHAPTER EIGHT

Humility and service

Knock, knock.

Who's there?

Jesus.

Jesus who?

Jesus who washed the feet of His disciples, even when they didn't expect it!

Anecdote: Jesus washed His disciples' feet to show that leadership is about serving others with humility.

Verse: "Now that I, your Lord and Teacher, have washed your feet, you also should wash one another's feet." (John 13:14)

Knock, knock.

Who's there?

Servant.

Servant who?

The servant King who rode into Jerusalem on a donkey!

Anecdote: Jesus entered Jerusalem humbly on a donkey, fulfilling prophecy and showing that His kingdom was about humility.

Verse: "See, your king comes to you, gentle and riding on a donkey." (Matthew 21:5)

Knock, knock.

Who's there?

Towel.

Towel who?

The towel Jesus used to dry the disciples' feet, showing humility in action.

Anecdote: Jesus used a towel to dry the disciples' feet after washing them, a humble act of service.

Verse: "He poured water into a basin and began to wash his disciples' feet." (John 13:5)

Knock, knock.

Who's there?

Least.

Least who?

The least among you will be the greatest, just as Jesus showed by serving others.

Anecdote: Jesus taught that those who serve humbly, like Him, are truly great in God's kingdom.

Verse: "The greatest among you will be your servant." (Matthew 23:11)

Knock, knock.
Who's there?
Crown.
Crown who?
The crown Jesus didn't take, because He came to serve, not to be served.

Anecdote: *Jesus came not for a royal crown but to serve humankind, a symbol of His humility.*
Verse: *"For even the Son of Man did not come to be served, but to serve." (Mark 10:45)*

Knock, knock.
Who's there?
Servant.
Servant who?
Servant of all, just like Jesus who became the servant of many.

Anecdote: *Jesus took on the role of a servant, putting others' needs before His own, the ultimate act of humility.*
Verse: *"Whoever wants to become great among you must be your servant." (Matthew 20:26)*

Knock, knock.
Who's there?
Table.
Table who?
The table Jesus flipped when He saw prideful hearts!

Anecdote: *Jesus overturned the tables of the money changers in the temple, showing that humility, not pride, belongs in God's house.*
Verse: *"Jesus entered the temple courts and drove out all who were buying and selling there." (Matthew 21:12)*

Knock, knock.
Who's there?
First.
First who?
The first will be last, and the last will be first—just like Jesus said!

Anecdote: *Jesus flipped the world's idea of greatness by saying the humble and the servant-hearted would be honored.*
Verse: *"So the last will be first, and the first will be last." (Matthew 20:16)*

Knock, knock.
Who's there?
Carpenter.
Carpenter who?
The humble carpenter who came to build hearts, not houses.

Anecdote: *Jesus worked as a humble carpenter, emphasizing His willingness to serve in everyday life.*
Verse: *"Isn't this the carpenter?" (Mark 6:3)*

Knock, knock.
Who's there?

Basin.

Basin who?

The basin of water Jesus used to wash His disciples' feet, teaching humility through service.

Anecdote: Jesus used a basin to wash His disciples' feet, a gesture of humility and love.
Verse: "After that, he poured water into a basin and began to wash his disciples' feet." (John 13:5)

Punny Jokes

Why didn't Jesus ever need a crown?
Because He was already the King of hearts!

Anecdote: Jesus chose humility over seeking worldly power, focusing on serving others instead of ruling them.
Verse: "For even the Son of Man did not come to be served, but to serve." (Mark 10:45)

Why did Jesus take up carpentry?
Because He always liked building bridges, not walls!

Anecdote: *As a carpenter, Jesus not only built things physically but spiritually, by bringing people together through His humble acts of love.*
Verse: *"Isn't this the carpenter?" (Mark 6:3)*

Why did Jesus wash His disciples' feet?
Because He wanted to show that being "sole-ful" was more important than being powerful!

Anecdote: *Jesus washed His disciples' feet as a humble act of service, teaching them the value of servanthood.*
Verse: *"Now that I, your Lord and Teacher, have washed your feet, you also should wash one another's feet." (John 13:14)*

Why didn't Jesus need a fancy donkey for His entry into Jerusalem?
Because He knew that being humble always gets you "a-head"!

Anecdote: *Jesus entered Jerusalem riding on a donkey, symbolizing His humility and peace.*
Verse: *"See, your king comes to you, gentle and riding on a donkey." (Matthew 21:5)*

What did Jesus say when the disciples argued about who was the greatest?
"Guys, it's not about being on top—it's about being at their feet!"

Anecdote: *Jesus taught His disciples that the greatest among them must be the servant of all, flipping the world's view of greatness.*
Verse: *"The greatest among you will be your servant." (Matthew 23:11)*

Why did Jesus never ask for a throne?
Because He preferred to reign in hearts, not in palaces!

Anecdote: *Jesus' kingdom wasn't about political power or thrones but about serving people and winning their hearts.*
Verse: *"My kingdom is not of this world." (John 18:36)*

Why did Jesus turn water into wine at the wedding?
Because He didn't just serve—He "poured" out His love for everyone!

Anecdote: *Jesus' first miracle at the wedding in Cana was not just about a supernatural event but also about serving others with love.*
Verse: *"He thus revealed his glory, and his disciples believed in him." (John 2:11)*

What's Jesus' favorite kind of leadership?
Servant-leadership, because it lifts others up instead of knocking them down!

Anecdote: *Jesus demonstrated servant-leadership by serving His followers, rather than expecting them to serve Him.*
Verse: *"Whoever wants to become great among you must be your servant." (Matthew 20:26)*

Why didn't Jesus mind being born in a stable?
Because He knew greatness starts from humble beginnings!

Anecdote: *Jesus' birth in a manger reflects His humility, even from the very start of His earthly life.*

Verse: *"She placed him in a manger, because there was no guest room available for them." (Luke 2:7)*

Why did Jesus carry a cross instead of a crown?
Because He knew that true kings don't wear jewels—they bear burdens for others!

Anecdote: *Jesus bore the cross for humanity, displaying the ultimate act of humble service.*

Verse: *"And being found in appearance as a man, he humbled himself by becoming obedient to death—even death on a cross!" (Philippians 2:8)*

One Liners Jokes

Jesus didn't need a throne; He preferred to wash feet instead!

Anecdote: *Jesus demonstrated humility by washing His disciples' feet, teaching that true greatness comes from serving others.*

Verse: *"Now that I, your Lord and Teacher, have washed your feet, you also should wash one another's feet." (John 13:14)*

Why did Jesus ride a donkey into Jerusalem? Because He knew a humble entrance beats a grand exit!

Anecdote: Jesus' humble entry fulfilled prophecy and showcased His mission of peace.
Verse: "See, your king comes to you, gentle and riding on a donkey." (Matthew 21:5)

Jesus was so humble, even His birth certificate was signed "Mary's Son"!

Anecdote: Jesus was born in a manger, showing that greatness can come from the most humble beginnings.
Verse: "She wrapped him in cloths and placed him in a manger." (Luke 2:7)

Jesus didn't carry a crown; He carried a cross—talk about a weighty decision!

Anecdote: Jesus chose to bear the cross for humanity, exemplifying selfless love and service.
Verse: "And being found in appearance as a man, he humbled himself by becoming obedient to death—even death on a cross!" (Philippians 2:8)

Why did Jesus prefer parables over PowerPoints? Because stories stick better when you serve them with love!
Anecdote: Jesus used parables to teach profound truths in relatable ways, showing His understanding of human hearts.
Verse: "He did not say anything to them without using a parable." (Mark 4:34)

Jesus was like a spiritual janitor, always cleaning up messes—talk about a servant leader!

Anecdote: *Jesus came to serve and not to be served, demonstrating the heart of a true leader.*
Verse: *"For even the Son of Man did not come to be served, but to serve." (Mark 10:45)*

Jesus taught us that when life gives you lemons, you make the best lemonade for others!

Anecdote: *Jesus always turned difficult situations into opportunities to serve and bless others.*
Verse: *"The greatest among you will be your servant." (Matthew 23:11)*

Why did Jesus always carry a towel? Because you never know when a foot-washing opportunity will arise!

Anecdote: *Jesus was always ready to serve, demonstrating that humility is about being prepared to help.*
Verse: *"He poured water into a basin and began to wash his disciples' feet." (John 13:5)*

Jesus proved that humility isn't a weakness—it's a superpower wrapped in love!

Anecdote: His humility empowered Him to connect deeply with people and transform lives.

Verse: "Humble yourselves before the Lord, and he will lift you up." (James 4:10)

Why did Jesus bring a fish to the party? Because He knew that sharing is caring!

Anecdote: *Jesus performed the miracle of feeding the 5,000, showing that serving others is the best way to celebrate.*

Verse: *"Jesus then took the loaves, gave thanks, and distributed to those who were seated." (John 6:11)*

Riddle jokes

I was born in a manger, humble and low,
With shepherds and wise men, I made quite a show.
Who am I?
Answer: Jesus!

Anecdote: Jesus' birth in a stable showed that true greatness often comes from the most humble beginnings.

Verse: "She wrapped him in cloths and placed him in a manger." (Luke 2:7)

I washed the feet of my friends one night,
To show them that serving is truly right.
What act did I perform?
Answer: Washing their feet!

Anecdote: Jesus washed His disciples' feet as an example of humility and servanthood.
Verse: "He began to wash his disciples' feet." (John 13:5)

I entered Jerusalem not on a horse,
But on a humble donkey, without much force.
Who am I?
Answer: Jesus!

Anecdote: *Jesus' choice of a donkey symbolized His mission of peace and humility.*
Verse: *"See, your king comes to you, gentle and riding on a donkey." (Matthew 21:5)*

I took five loaves and two fish, it's true,
To feed a crowd of thousands, what could I do?
What miracle did I perform?
Answer: Feeding the 5,000!

Anecdote: *Jesus multiplied the loaves and fish, demonstrating His love for the people and His ability to serve abundantly.*
Verse: *"Jesus then took the loaves, gave thanks, and distributed to those who were seated." (John 6:11)*

I said, "Let the little children come to me,"
Showing that service is for all, you see.
Who am I?
Answer: Jesus!

Anecdote: Jesus welcomed children, highlighting that everyone is valuable in His eyes.
Verse: "Let the little children come to me, and do not hinder them." (Mark 10:14)

I didn't wear a crown, but I wore a towel,
To show my disciples how to serve and not scowl.
What did I use?
Answer: A towel!

Anecdote: Jesus wrapped a towel around Himself to wash His disciples' feet, exemplifying servant leadership.
Verse: "He wrapped a towel around his waist." (John 13:4)

When people asked, "Who's the greatest of all?"
I said, "Be like a servant; answer the call."
What lesson did I teach?
Answer: Humility in service!

Anecdote: Jesus taught that greatness comes from serving others, not from seeking power.
Verse: "The greatest among you will be your servant." (Matthew 23:11)

I turned water into wine at a party so fine,
To serve joy and love, making life divine.
What miracle did I perform?
Answer: Turning water into wine!

Anecdote: This miracle at the wedding in Cana showed Jesus' willingness to serve and bring joy to others.
Verse: "Jesus performed this first miracle at Cana in Galilee." (John 2:11)

I told parables to teach with ease,
With stories and lessons that aim to please.
What method did I use?
Answer: Parables!

Anecdote: Jesus often used parables to convey profound truths, making them relatable and memorable.
Verse: "He did not say anything to them without using a parable." (Mark 4:34)

I was known to share food and love,
With my disciples and crowds—blessings from above.
What did I do?
Answer: Served food and shared love!

Anecdote: Jesus consistently served others, showcasing the importance of love and community.
Verse: "He took the bread, gave thanks, broke it, and gave it to them." (Luke 22:19)

PART THREE

Jesus and His Followers

CHAPTER NINE

Disciples and apostles

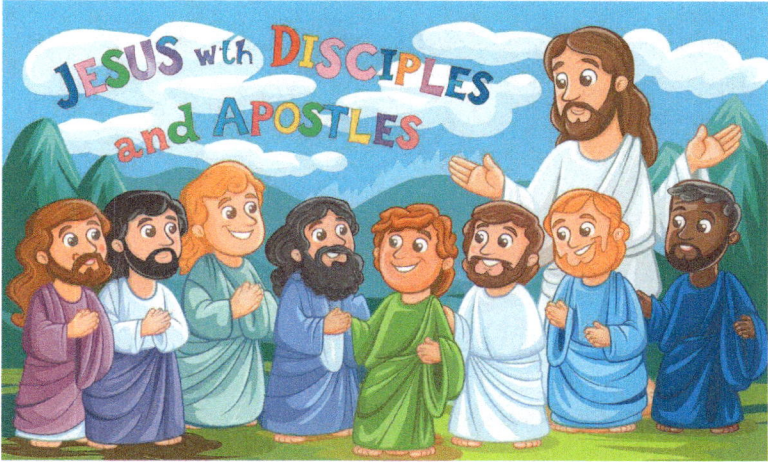

Knock, knock.

Who's there?

Peter.

Peter who?

Peter up your nets; we're going fishing!

Anecdote: Jesus called Peter and his brother Andrew while they were fishing and invited them to be "fishers of men."

Verse: "Follow me, and I will send you out to fish for people." (Matthew 4:19)

Knock, knock.

Who's there?

James.

James who?

James and John, the sons of thunder, here to shake things up!

Anecdote: Jesus nicknamed James and John "Sons of Thunder" due to their passionate nature.
Verse: "James son of Zebedee and his brother John (they were together called Sons of Thunder)." (Mark 3:17)

Knock, knock.
Who's there?
Matthew.
Matthew who?
Matthew you need to follow Jesus to find your purpose!

Anecdote: Matthew was a tax collector who left everything to follow Jesus.
Verse: "He saw a man named Matthew sitting at the tax collector's booth. 'Follow me,' he told him." (Matthew 9:9)

Knock, knock.
Who's there?
Thomas.
Thomas who?
Thomas the twin who just wanted to see to believe!

Anecdote: Thomas doubted Jesus' resurrection until he saw Him and touched His wounds.
Verse: "Unless I see the nail marks in his hands, I will not believe." (John 20:25)

Knock, knock.
Who's there?
Judas.
Judas who?
Judas want to betray Jesus? No way, not me!

Anecdote: Judas Iscariot is known for betraying Jesus for thirty pieces of silver.
Verse: "Then Judas Iscariot, one of the Twelve, went to the chief priests to betray Jesus to them." (Matthew 26:14)

Knock, knock.
Who's there?
Simon.
Simon who?
Simon says to take up your cross and follow Him!

Anecdote: Jesus emphasized the need for self-denial and following Him.
Verse: "Whoever wants to be my disciple must deny themselves and take up their cross." (Mark 8:34)

Knock, knock.
Who's there?
Andrew.
Andrew who?
Andrew's brother, Peter, brought me along!

Anecdote: Andrew was Peter's brother and the first disciple Jesus called.
Verse: "He first found his own brother Simon and told him, 'We have found the Messiah.'" (John 1:41)

Knock, knock.
Who's there?
Philip.
Philip who?
Philip your heart with love; Jesus is here!

Anecdote: *Philip was enthusiastic about spreading the message of Jesus.*
Verse: *"Philip found Nathanael and told him, 'We have found the one Moses wrote about in the Law.'" (John 1:45)*

Knock, knock.
Who's there?
Bartholomew.
Bartholomew who?
Bartholomew you're the one who has seen the true light!

Anecdote: *Bartholomew (Nathanael) was known for his straightforward nature and faith in Jesus.*
Verse: *"Here truly is an Israelite in whom there is no deceit." (John 1:47)*

Knock, knock.
Who's there?
Matthew.
Matthew who?
Matthew we need to spread the good news!

Anecdote: Matthew's Gospel emphasizes spreading Jesus' teachings.
Verse: "Go therefore and make disciples of all nations." (Matthew 28:19)

Punny Jokes

Joke: Why did Peter always carry a pencil?
Answer: Because he wanted to draw closer to Jesus!

Anecdote: Peter was one of the first disciples called by Jesus, demonstrating a desire to be close to Him.
Verse: "Come, follow me," Jesus said, "and I will send you out to fish for people." (Matthew 4:19)

Joke: What did Jesus say to the fisherman who was always late?
Answer: "Time to scale back on your excuses!"

Anecdote: Jesus called fishermen to be His disciples, showing that He valued their skills and commitment.
Verse: "Follow me, and I will make you fishers of men." (Matthew 4:19)

Joke: Why was Matthew the best tax collector?

Answer: Because he always knew how to "balance" the books!

Anecdote: Matthew was a tax collector before becoming a disciple, illustrating how Jesus can transform anyone.
Verse: "As Jesus went on from there, he saw a man named Matthew sitting at the tax collector's booth." (Matthew 9:9)

Joke: Why did Thomas bring a ladder to meet Jesus?
Answer: Because he heard Jesus was going to raise the bar!

Anecdote: Thomas struggled with doubt but ultimately affirmed his faith in Jesus after seeing Him resurrected.
Verse: "My Lord and my God!" (John 20:28)

Joke: What did the disciples say when they had trouble finding food?
Answer: "Let's 'break' for bread!"

Anecdote: Jesus fed the 5,000, teaching the disciples about trust and provision.
Verse: "Jesus took the loaves, gave thanks, and distributed to those who were seated." (John 6:11)

Joke: How did Jesus feel when Peter denied Him?
Answer: He was "Peter-fied!"

Anecdote: Peter denied knowing Jesus three times, but he later repented and became a bold leader in the early church.
Verse: "Before the rooster crows, you will disown me three times." (John 18:27)

Joke: Why did the disciples always carry a map?
Answer: Because they wanted to know the "way" to Jesus!

Anecdote: Jesus taught that He is the way, the truth, and the life, guiding His followers in their journey.
Verse: "I am the way and the truth and the life." (John 14:6)

Joke: What did the disciples say to each other after Jesus healed the blind man?
Answer: "Now that's what I call 'sight' for sore eyes!"

Anecdote: Jesus performed many miracles, including healing the blind, showcasing His compassion and power.
Verse: "Jesus healed a man who had been blind from birth." (John 9:1)

Joke: Why did Judas always bring a pencil to meetings?
Answer: Because he wanted to make sure he had a "point" to betray!

Anecdote: Judas Iscariot is known for betraying Jesus, a somber reminder of loyalty and trust.
Verse: "Judas Iscariot, one of the Twelve, went to the chief priests to betray Jesus." (Mark 14:10)

Joke: What do you call it when the disciples have a disagreement?
Answer: A "cross"-examination!

Anecdote: *The disciples had their differences but learned to work together in spreading Jesus' message.*
Verse: *"They argued about who was the greatest among them." (Luke 9:46)*

One Liner Joke

Joke: Peter walked on water, but he couldn't swim in doubt!

Anecdote: *Peter's faith allowed him to walk on water, but he began to sink when doubt crept in.*
Verse: *"But when he saw the wind, he was afraid and, beginning to sink, cried out, 'Lord, save me!'" (Matthew 14:30)*

Joke: Matthew's favorite exercise? Tax evasion!

Anecdote: *Before following Jesus, Matthew was a tax collector, showing that Jesus calls everyone, even those with less-than-perfect pasts.*
Verse: *"Matthew, sitting at the tax collector's booth." (Matthew 9:9)*

Joke: Thomas couldn't find his way until he saw the light—literally!

Anecdote: *Thomas doubted Jesus' resurrection until he touched His wounds, proving that seeing is believing for him.*
Verse: *"Blessed are those who have not seen and yet have believed." (John 20:29)*

Joke: Judas thought he could cash in on betrayal, but he ended up bankrupt!

Anecdote: *Judas Iscariot betrayed Jesus for thirty pieces of silver, only to regret his decision.*
Verse: *"What are you willing to give me if I hand him over to you?" (Matthew 26:15)*

Joke: When the disciples debated who was the greatest, Jesus just rolled His eyes—He knew it was Him!

Anecdote: *The disciples often argued about their status among one another, revealing their human nature.*
Verse: *"They argued about who was the greatest among them." (Luke 9:46)*

Joke: Why did Philip always carry a notebook? He wanted to jot down every miraculous lesson!

Anecdote: *Philip was eager to spread the word of Jesus and shared the good news with others.*
Verse: *"Philip found Nathanael and told him, 'We have found the one Moses wrote about.'" (John 1:45)*

Joke: Bartholomew was the quiet one in the group—he just let his actions speak for themselves!

Anecdote: *Bartholomew (Nathanael) was known for his honesty and straightforwardness in his faith.*
Verse: *"Here truly is an Israelite in whom there is no deceit." (John 1:47)*

Joke: Why did the disciples bring a ladder to see Jesus? They heard He was raising the bar!

Anecdote*: Jesus consistently challenged His followers to elevate their understanding and actions.*
Verse: *"If anyone wants to be first, he must be the very last, and the servant of all." (Mark 9:35)*

Joke: Peter was great at fishing, but he didn't know how to catch a break!

Anecdote: *Peter was called from his fishing life to become a "fisher of men."*
Verse: *"Follow me, and I will make you fishers of men." (Matthew 4:19)*

Joke: Jesus had the best team—He just couldn't find a good manager!

Anecdote: *The disciples had their ups and downs, but Jesus guided them through every challenge.*
Verse: *"I have not come to call the righteous, but sinners to repentance." (Luke 5:32)*

Riddle Jokes

Riddle: I walked on water, but I didn't bring my swimming gear. Who am I?
Answer: Peter!

Anecdote: Peter demonstrated great faith by walking on water towards Jesus but began to sink when doubt filled his heart.
Verse: "Peter replied, 'Lord, if it's you, tell me to come to you on the water.'" (Matthew 14:28)

Riddle: I was a tax collector turned disciple. Who am I?
Answer: Matthew!

Anecdote: Matthew left his lucrative job to follow Jesus, showing that everyone can have a fresh start.
Verse: "Matthew got up and followed him." (Matthew 9:9)

Riddle: I doubted but later believed when I touched the wounds. Who am I?
Answer: Thomas!

Anecdote: Thomas' journey from doubt to faith highlights the importance of belief, even in uncertainty.
Verse: "Unless I see the nail marks in his hands... I will not believe." (John 20:25)

Riddle: I was the one who betrayed Jesus for thirty pieces of silver. Who am I?

Answer: Judas!

Anecdote: *Judas' betrayal serves as a warning about the dangers of greed and the impact of choices.*
Verse: *"Then Judas Iscariot, one of the Twelve, went to the chief priests to betray Jesus."*
(Mark 14:10)

Riddle: I wanted to see who Jesus was, but I had to climb a tree. Who am I?
Answer: Zacchaeus!

Anecdote: *Zacchaeus' determination to see Jesus illustrates the lengths people will go to encounter Him.*
Verse: *"Zacchaeus was a short man, and he could not see over the crowd." (Luke 19:3)*

Riddle: I'm known for being honest and straightforward, and I'm also one of the Twelve. Who am I?
Answer: Nathanael (Bartholomew)!

Anecdote: *Nathanael's encounter with Jesus shows that genuine seekers will find truth in Him.*
Verse: *"Here truly is an Israelite in whom there is no deceit." (John 1:47)*

Riddle: I used to be a fisherman but became a "fisher of men." Who am I?
Answer: Peter!

Anecdote: Peter's transformation exemplifies how Jesus calls people to a higher purpose.

Verse: "I will make you fishers of men." (Matthew 4:19)

Riddle: I walked with Jesus, but I often wondered who was the greatest. Who am I?
Answer: The disciples!

Anecdote: The disciples often debated their status, revealing human nature's struggles with pride.
Verse: "They came to Capernaum. When he was in the house, he asked them, 'What were you arguing about on the road?'" (Mark 9:33)

Riddle: I had five loaves and two fish, and I helped feed thousands. Who am I?
Answer: A boy (the boy with the lunch)!

Anecdote: This story teaches that even small contributions can lead to great miracles when given to Jesus.
Verse: "Here is a boy with five small barley loaves and two small fish." (John 6:9)

Riddle: I said, "Lord, if it's you, tell me to come to you on the water." Who am I?
Answer: Peter!

Anecdote: Peter's faith led him to step out onto the water, showing the importance of trusting in Jesus.
Verse: "'Come,' he said. Then Peter got down out of the boat, walked on the water, and came toward Jesus." (Matthew 14:29)

CHAPTER TEN

Early Church

Knock, knock.
Who's there?
Peter.
Peter who?
Peter the rock, the Church is built on me!

Anecdote: Jesus called Peter "the rock" on which He would build His Church, highlighting Peter's foundational role.
Verse: "And I tell you that you are Peter, and on this rock, I will build my church." (Matthew 16:18)

Knock, knock.

Who's there?
James.
James who?
James the just, leading the early Church with wisdom!

Anecdote: James, the brother of Jesus, became a key leader in the early Church in Jerusalem.
Verse: "James, a servant of God and of the Lord Jesus Christ." (James 1:1)

Knock, knock.
Who's there?
Paul.
Paul who?
Paul-ishing the gospel to all nations!

Anecdote: Paul, formerly Saul, became a passionate apostle, spreading the Gospel across the Roman Empire.
Verse: "Therefore go and make disciples of all nations." (Matthew 28:19)

Knock, knock.
Who's there?
John.
John who?
John the beloved, always ready for a love letter!

Anecdote: John is known for his close relationship with Jesus and for writing several New Testament books emphasizing love.
Verse: "Dear friends, let us love one another." (1 John 4:7)

Knock, knock.

Who's there?

Barnabas.

Barnabas who?

Barnabas the encourager, spreading joy in the early Church!

Anecdote: Barnabas was known for his encouragement and support of the apostles, particularly Paul.

Verse: "Joseph, a Levite from Cyprus, whom the apostles called Barnabas." (Acts 4:36)

Knock, knock.

Who's there?

Lydia.

Lydia who?

Lydia the seller of purple, bringing color to the early Church!

Anecdote: Lydia was a businesswoman who became one of the first converts in Europe, hosting Paul and the apostles.

Verse: "The Lord opened her heart to respond to Paul's message." (Acts 16:14)

Knock, knock.

Who's there?

Stephen.

Stephen who?

Stephen the first martyr, standing strong in faith!

Anecdote: Stephen was the first Christian martyr, known for his bold testimony and faith in the face of persecution.

Verse: "They stoned Stephen, calling on God." (Acts 7:59)

Knock, knock.

Who's there?

Philip.

Philip who?

Philip the evangelist, spreading the good news everywhere!

Anecdote: Philip preached to many, including the Ethiopian eunuch, showing the early Church's mission to reach all people.

Verse: "Philip began with that very passage of Scripture and told him the good news about Jesus." (Acts 8:35)

Knock, knock.

Who's there?

Timothy.

Timothy who?

Timothy the faithful, always ready to help!

Knock, knock.

Who's there?

Church.

Church who?

Church is where we all gather to share the love of Jesus!

Anecdote: *The early Church met regularly for teaching, fellowship, and breaking bread together, embodying community and love.*
Verse: *"They devoted themselves to the apostles' teaching and to fellowship." (Acts 2:42)*

Punny Jokes

Joke: Why did Peter always carry a pencil?
Because he wanted to draw people to Christ!

Anecdote: Peter was known for his powerful preaching, bringing many to faith.
Verse: "And the Lord added to their number daily those who were being saved."
(Acts 2:47)

Joke: Why was Paul such a good letter writer?
Because he always delivered the "mail" of good news!

Anecdote: *Paul wrote many letters (epistles) to the early churches, encouraging them in their faith.*
Verse: *"Grace and peace to you from God our Father and the Lord Jesus Christ."*
(Romans 1:7)

Joke: Why did Lydia start a clothing line?
Because she was great at dyeing to sell purple!

Anecdote: *Lydia was a successful seller of purple goods and became an early convert.*
Verse: *"She was a dealer in purple cloth from the city of Thyatira." (Acts 16:14)*

Joke: Why was Timothy always calm?
Because he had the spirit of a true believer!

Anecdote: *Timothy was known for his sincere faith and dedication.*
Verse: *"For God has not given us a spirit of fear, but of power, love, and a sound mind." (2 Timothy 1:7)*

Joke: Why did the early church love potlucks?
Because they believed in sharing the bread of life!

Anecdote: *The early Christians often shared meals and broke bread together as part of their fellowship.*
Verse: *"They broke bread in their homes and ate together with glad and sincere hearts." (Acts 2:46)*

Joke: Why did John bring a ladder to the church?
Because he wanted to reach new heights in faith!
Anecdote: *John is often regarded as a deep thinker and theologian among the apostles.*
Verse: *"To him who is able to do immeasurably more than all we ask or imagine." (Ephesians 3:20)*

Joke: Why did Stephen always stay positive?
Because he had a stone-cold faith!

Anecdote: Stephen, the first martyr, remained faithful even in the face of persecution.
Verse: "But Stephen, full of the Holy Spirit, looked up to heaven and saw the glory of God." (Acts 7:55)

Joke: Why did the apostles never get lost?
Because they always followed the way!

Anecdote: The early Christians were known as followers of "the Way," referring to their following of Jesus.
Verse: "I am the way, the truth, and the life." (John 14:6)

Joke: Why did Barnabas open a support group?
Because he believed in lifting others up!

Anecdote: Barnabas was known for his encouragement and support of Paul and others in the early Church.
Verse: "He was a good man, full of the Holy Spirit and faith." (Acts 11:24)

Joke: Why did the early Church start a bakery?
Because they wanted to spread the good yeast!

Anecdote: *The early Church was known for sharing and spreading the Gospel, like leavening spreading through dough.*
Verse: *"A little yeast works through the whole batch of dough." (Galatians 5:9)*

One Liners Jokes

Joke: Peter walked on water, but he always said, "It's not my fault if I sink; I just can't help but float my boat!"

Anecdote: *Peter was known for his faith and his moments of doubt while walking on water.*
Verse: *"But when he saw the wind, he was afraid and, beginning to sink, cried out, 'Lord, save me!'" (Matthew 14:30)*

Joke: Paul didn't need a GPS; he just followed the Holy Spirit's directions!

Anecdote: *Paul was led by the Spirit to spread the Gospel far and wide, often encountering challenges along the way.*
Verse: *"The Holy Spirit said to them, 'Set apart for me Barnabas and Saul for the work to which I have called them.'" (Acts 13:2)*

Joke: The early church knew how to keep things current—they had the best "flow" of the Spirit!

Anecdote: *The early Church was characterized by the outpouring of the Holy Spirit at Pentecost, empowering them to spread the Gospel.*
Verse: *"When the day of Pentecost came, they were all together in one place." (Acts 2:1)*

Joke: John's favorite job? Being the beloved disciple—it's a "role" he really cherished!

Anecdote: *John is known for his close relationship with Jesus and for emphasizing love in his writings.*
Verse: *"This is the disciple who testifies to these things and who wrote them down. We know that his testimony is true." (John 21:24)*

Joke: Timothy always knew how to tackle tough problems—he had Paul to guide him!

Anecdote: *Timothy was mentored by Paul and became a key leader in the early Church, known for his faith and dedication.*
Verse: *"I have no one else like him, who takes a genuine interest in your welfare."* (Philippians 2:20)

Joke: Why did the early Christians excel at networking? They really knew how to connect with the Spirit!

Anecdote: *The early Church thrived on community, sharing everything and supporting one another in their faith.*

Verse: *"They devoted themselves to the apostles' teaching and to fellowship." (Acts 2:42)*

Joke: Why was Barnabas always in high spirits? Because he was the ultimate encourager!

Anecdote: Barnabas was known for uplifting others and played a significant role in supporting Paul and others.
Verse: "He was a good man, full of the Holy Spirit and faith." (Acts 11:24)

Joke: Why did the early Church love sharing meals? They believed in breaking bread and not hearts!

Anecdote: The early Christians often shared meals together, fostering community and love among believers.
Verse: "They broke bread in their homes and ate together with glad and sincere hearts." (Acts 2:46)

Joke: Why was Stephen always in good spirits? Because he was stoned for his faith!

Anecdote: Stephen was the first martyr of the Christian faith, known for his unwavering conviction.
Verse: "While they were stoning him, Stephen prayed, 'Lord Jesus, receive my spirit.'" (Acts 7:59)

Joke: The early Christians didn't just spread the Word; they fished for souls!

Anecdote: Many of Jesus' followers, like Peter, were fishermen called to become "fishers of men."

Verse: "Come, follow me, and I will send you out to fish for people." (Matthew 4:19)

Riddles Jokes

Riddle: I was a fisherman who became a rock; I walked on water, and I couldn't be stopped. Who am I?

Answer: Peter!

Anecdote: Peter was called by Jesus to be a disciple and played a pivotal role in the early Church.

Verse: "And I tell you that you are Peter, and on this rock, I will build my church." (Matthew 16:18)

Riddle: I wrote letters to guide the early flock, my travels spread the Word around the block. Who am I?

Answer: Paul!

Anecdote: Paul traveled extensively to spread the Gospel and wrote many epistles to encourage the churches.

Verse: "I have become all things to all people so that by all possible means I might save some." (1 Corinthians 9:22)

Riddle: I preached to the crowds and baptized many, my name means "beloved," and I was never petty. Who am I?
Answer: John!

Anecdote: John was known as the beloved disciple and wrote the Gospel that bears his name.
Verse: "This is the disciple who testifies to these things and who wrote them down." (John 21:24)

Riddle: I was a seller of purple, my heart was true; when I met Paul, I knew what to do. Who am I?
Answer: Lydia!
Anecdote: Lydia was a successful businesswoman who became one of the first converts in Europe.
Verse: "The Lord opened her heart to respond to Paul's message." (Acts 16:14)

Riddle: I stood by as they threw stones, but I never ran; I asked God to forgive them, just as Jesus ran. Who am I?
Answer: Stephen!

Anecdote: Stephen was the first Christian martyr and remained faithful even to the end.
Verse: "Then he fell on his knees and cried out, 'Lord, do not hold this sin against them.'" (Acts 7:60)

Riddle: I was a young leader, taught by a great man; my faith and courage helped the church expand. Who am I?
Answer: Timothy!

Anecdote: Timothy was mentored by Paul and became a key figure in the early Church.
Verse: "For God has not given us a spirit of fear, but of power and of love and of a sound mind." (2 Timothy 1:7)

Riddle: I fed the hungry and healed the lame; in the name of Jesus, I spread His fame. Who am I?
Answer: The apostles!

Anecdote: The apostles performed many miracles in Jesus' name, helping to spread His message.
Verse: "The apostles performed many signs and wonders among the people." (Acts 5:12)

Riddle: I am a group that meets to share and pray, our love for each other grows stronger each day. Who are we?
Answer: The early Church!

Anecdote: The early Christians met regularly for fellowship, prayer, and breaking bread.
Verse: "They devoted themselves to the apostles' teaching and to fellowship." (Acts 2:42)

Riddle: I was known for my encouragement and my good deeds; I helped the early believers with their needs. Who am I?
Answer: Barnabas!

Anecdote: Barnabas played a crucial role in encouraging Paul and supporting the early Christians.
Verse: "He was a good man, full of the Holy Spirit and faith." (Acts 11:24)

Riddle: I was called to pray and lead, my faith was strong, and I took the lead. Who am I?
Answer: The deacons!

Anecdote: The early Church appointed deacons to help with the distribution of food and care for the community.
Verse: "They chose Stephen, a man full of faith and of the Holy Spirit." (Acts 6:5)

PART FOUR

Comparing Jesus to Others

CHAPTER ELEVEN

Jesus vs. other historical figures

Knock, knock.

Who's there?

Moses.

Moses who?

Moses never made it to the Promised Land, but Jesus opens the way to heaven!

Anecdote: *Moses led the Israelites to the Promised Land but wasn't allowed to enter. Jesus offers eternal life through His sacrifice.*

Verse: *"I am the way and the truth and the life." (John 14:6)*

Knock, knock.
Who's there?
Caesar.
Caesar who?
Caesar's kingdom is temporary, but Jesus' reign is eternal!

Anecdote: *While Caesar ruled with power, Jesus taught about a heavenly kingdom that lasts forever.*
Verse: *"My kingdom is not of this world." (John 18:36)*

Knock, knock.
Who's there?
Einstein.
Einstein who?
Einstein might be smart, but Jesus is the wisdom of God!

Anecdote: *Jesus, in His teachings, displayed wisdom beyond comprehension, teaching profound truths.*
Verse: *"In whom are hidden all the treasures of wisdom and knowledge." (Colossians 2:3)*

Knock, knock.
Who's there?
Buddha.
Buddha who?
Buddha said to seek enlightenment, but Jesus says, "I am the light of the world!"

Anecdote: *Jesus refers to Himself as the light, guiding believers in truth and righteousness.*

Verse: *"I am the light of the world." (John 8:12)*

Knock, knock.

Who's there?

Socrates.

Socrates who?

Socrates asked questions, but Jesus is the answer!

Anecdote: *Jesus answered the deep questions of life and provided clarity and truth to those seeking understanding.*

Verse: *"I am the way and the truth." (John 14:6)*

Knock, knock.

Who's there?

Confucius.

Confucius who?

Confucius says, "He who finds truth finds peace," but Jesus says, "Peace I leave with you!"

Anecdote: *Jesus offers a peace that surpasses understanding, unlike any wisdom of the world.*

Verse: *"Peace I leave with you; my peace I give you." (John 14:27)*

Knock, knock.

Who's there?

Alexander.

Alexander who?

Alexander conquered lands, but Jesus conquers hearts!

Anecdote: Unlike earthly rulers, Jesus transforms lives and reigns in the hearts of His followers.
Verse: "For the kingdom of God is not a matter of talk but of power." (1 Corinthians 4:20)

Knock, knock.
Who's there?
Plato.
Plato who?
Plato had theories, but Jesus is the truth made flesh!

Anecdote: Jesus embodies truth, unlike philosophical ideas that can be debated.
Verse: "The Word became flesh and made his dwelling among us." (John 1:14)

Knock, knock.
Who's there?
Martin Luther.
Martin Luther who?
Martin Luther fought for faith, but Jesus is the founder of our faith!

Anecdote: Jesus is the cornerstone of Christianity, the one who paved the way for our salvation.
Verse: "Jesus is the author and perfecter of our faith." (Hebrews 12:2)

Knock, knock.

Who's there?

Mother Teresa.

Mother Teresa who?

Mother Teresa showed love, but Jesus is love personified!

Anecdote: Jesus' life exemplifies love in its purest form, guiding us to love one another.
Verse: "God is love." (1 John 4:8)

Punny Jokes

1.

Joke: Why did Jesus break up with Caesar?

Because he wanted a "real" relationship, not just a "Roman" holiday!

Anecdote: Jesus emphasized genuine relationships built on love and truth, unlike political alliances.
Verse: "This is my command: Love each other." (John 15:17)

Joke: Why didn't Jesus need a GPS?

Because He was the "way" before they even invented directions!

Anecdote: Jesus described Himself as the way to eternal life, guiding us on the right path.
Verse: "I am the way and the truth and the life." (John 14:6)

Joke: What did Buddha say to Jesus?

"Let's meditate on how to make the world a better place, but I think you've got it covered!"

Anecdote: *Jesus' teachings focus on love and compassion, showing us the path to a better world.*

Verse: *"Love your neighbor as yourself." (Mark 12:31)*

Joke: Why did Socrates want to hang out with Jesus?
Because he heard Jesus had all the best "answers"!

Anecdote: *Jesus answered the tough questions about life, providing wisdom beyond human understanding.*
Verse: *"In him are hidden all the treasures of wisdom and knowledge." (Colossians 2:3)*

Joke: Why did Alexander the Great admire Jesus?
Because Jesus conquered hearts without ever raising a sword!

Anecdote: *Jesus' influence spreads through love and compassion, unlike military conquests.*
Verse: *"For the kingdom of God is not a matter of talk but of power." (1 Corinthians 4:20)*

Joke: What did Martin Luther say about Jesus?
"He really nailed it on the cross, didn't he?"

Anecdote: Jesus' sacrifice on the cross was pivotal for salvation, making a lasting impact on faith.
Verse: "He himself bore our sins in his body on the tree." (1 Peter 2:24)

Joke: Why did Mother Teresa invite Jesus to her charity event?
Because she knew He was the "best at giving" without expecting anything back!

Anecdote: Jesus taught selfless giving and love for the poor and needy.
Verse: "It is more blessed to give than to receive." (Acts 20:35)

Joke: Why did Einstein study Jesus?
Because he wanted to understand the "light" that shone through Him!

Anecdote: Jesus referred to Himself as the light of the world, illuminating the path to truth.
Verse: "I am the light of the world." (John 8:12)

Joke: What did Confucius say after reading the Gospels?
"I guess I should've been more 'confident' in what I said about kindness!"

Anecdote: Jesus taught kindness and love, reinforcing the value of treating others well.
Verse: "Do to others as you would have them do to you." (Luke 6:31)

Joke: Why did Plato think Jesus was special?
Because He was the only one who could truly define "the good"!

Anecdote: *Jesus embodied goodness and righteousness, showing us the way to live.*
Verse: *"No one is good—except God alone." (Mark 10:18)*

One Liner Jokes

Joke: Jesus didn't need a throne; He ruled the hearts of His followers!

Anecdote: *Unlike earthly kings, Jesus reigns through love and compassion.*
Verse: *"The kingdom of God is within you." (Luke 17:21)*

Joke: Caesar might have conquered nations, but Jesus conquered sin!

Anecdote: *Jesus' victory over sin and death offers salvation to all.*
Verse: *"For the wages of sin is death, but the gift of God is eternal life." (Romans 6:23)*

Joke: While Socrates asked questions, Jesus provided all the answers!

Anecdote: *Jesus brought clarity and truth to life's biggest questions.*
Verse: *"I am the way and the truth and the life." (John 14:6)*

Joke: Buddha found peace, but Jesus is the Prince of Peace!

Anecdote: *Jesus offers a peace that transcends all understanding.*
Verse: *"Peace I leave with you; my peace I give you." (John 14:27)*

Joke: Einstein may have had theories, but Jesus is the ultimate truth!

Anecdote: *Jesus embodies the truth of God's love and purpose for humanity.*
Verse: *"In him are hidden all the treasures of wisdom and knowledge." (Colossians 2:3)*

Joke: While Alexander the Great sought glory, Jesus sought the lost!

Anecdote: *Jesus' mission was to save those in need, not to seek fame.*
Verse: *"For the Son of Man came to seek and to save the lost." (Luke 19:10)*

Joke: Mother Teresa helped the poor, but Jesus is the source of all compassion!

Anecdote: *Jesus demonstrated perfect love and compassion throughout His life.*
Verse: *"God is love." (1 John 4:8)*

Joke: Plato had ideals, but Jesus is the ideal!

Anecdote: *Jesus embodies the perfection of goodness, righteousness, and love.*
Verse: *"No one is good—except God alone." (Mark 10:18)*

Joke: Confucius taught kindness, but Jesus lived it out every day!

Anecdote: *Jesus' life was a testament to love and kindness towards all.*
Verse: *"Do to others as you would have them do to you." (Luke 6:31)*

Joke: Martin Luther sparked a reformation, but Jesus initiated the transformation!

Anecdote: *Jesus' sacrifice changed the course of history and the hearts of believers.*
Verse: *"If anyone is in Christ, he is a new creation." (2 Corinthians 5:17)*

Riddle Jokes

Riddle: I taught many lessons and walked on water too,
But I didn't need a throne to rule over you.
Who am I?
Answer: Jesus

Anecdote: *Jesus performed miracles to demonstrate His divine authority and love.*
Verse: *"Jesus replied, 'You do not realize now what I am doing, but later you will understand.'" (John 13:7)*

Riddle: I conquered nations and ruled with might,
But one man's sacrifice brought eternal light.
Who am I?

Answer: Caesar

Anecdote: Jesus' sacrifice on the cross offers salvation, unlike any earthly power.
Verse: "For God so loved the world that he gave his one and only Son." (John 3:16)

Riddle: I sought wisdom through questions, deep and profound,
But in the end, the answer in me can be found.
Who am I?
Answer: Socrates

Anecdote: Jesus provided clarity and wisdom, revealing truths that transformed lives.
Verse: "You will know the truth, and the truth will set you free." (John 8:32)

Riddle: I taught about suffering and finding peace within,
But my followers found solace through Him.
Who am I?
Answer: Buddha

Anecdote: Jesus offers true peace through His love and grace.
Verse: "Come to me, all you who are weary and burdened, and I will give you rest."
(Matthew 11:28)

Riddle: I pondered the universe with theories so bright,
Yet the greatest truth shines in the world's Light.
Who am I?
Answer: Einstein

Anecdote: Jesus is the light that guides and reveals the truth of God.
Verse: "I am the light of the world." (John 8:12)

Riddle: I sought glory with an army, fierce and grand,
But one humble man showed love to all the land.
Who am I?
Answer: Alexander the Great

Anecdote: Jesus' mission was to save the lost, not to seek power.
Verse: "For the Son of Man came to seek and to save the lost." (Luke 19:10)

Riddle: I served the poor with compassion and grace,
But the true source of love came to take my place.
Who am I?
Answer: Mother Teresa

Anecdote: Jesus exemplified perfect compassion throughout His ministry.
Verse: "God is love." (1 John 4:8)

Riddle: I had ideals about goodness, virtue, and fate,
But the embodiment of truth came to demonstrate.
Who am I?
Answer: Plato
Anecdote: Jesus lived out the ideals of goodness and righteousness.
Verse: "No one is good—except God alone." (Mark 10:18)

Riddle:

I spoke of kindness, wisdom, and peace,

Yet my life taught love that would never cease.

Who am I?

Answer: Confucius

Anecdote: Jesus' teachings on love resonate with the heart of His message.

Verse: "Do to others as you would have them do to you." (Luke 6:31)

Riddle: I sparked a movement with my 95 Theses,

But the man who loves unconditionally never ceases.

Who am I?

Answer: Martin Luther

Anecdote: Jesus' message transformed hearts and lives, ushering in a new covenant.

Verse: "If anyone is in Christ, he is a new creation." (2 Corinthians 5:17)

CHAPTER TWELVE

Jesus vs. fictional characters

Knock, knock.
Who's there?
Jesus.
Jesus who?
Jesus, the original superhero who doesn't wear a cape!

Anecdote: Jesus performed miraculous healings and teachings, showcasing His divine power.
Verse: "For I have not come to call the righteous, but sinners." (Matthew 9:13)

Knock, knock.
Who's there?
Hercules.

Hercules who?

Hercules may have strength, but Jesus has the power to save!

Anecdote: While Hercules is known for his physical strength, Jesus demonstrated ultimate strength through love and sacrifice.

Verse: "Greater love has no one than this: to lay down one's life for one's friends." (John 15:13)

Knock, knock.

Who's there?

Batman.

Batman who?

Batman saves Gotham, but Jesus saves the world!

Anecdote: Jesus came to offer salvation to all, while Batman fights crime in one city.

Verse: "For the Son of Man came to seek and to save the lost." (Luke 19:10)

Knock, knock.

Who's there?

Frodo.

Frodo who?

Frodo carried a ring, but Jesus carries our burdens!

Anecdote: Just as Frodo bore the burden of the One Ring, Jesus bore our sins on the cross.

Verse: "Come to me, all you who are weary and burdened, and I will give you rest." (Matthew 11:28)

Knock, knock.

Who's there?

Yoda.

Yoda who?

Yoda may be wise, but Jesus is the Way!

Anecdote: *Yoda offers wisdom, but Jesus provides the path to eternal life.*
Verse: *"I am the way and the truth and the life." (John 14:6)*

Knock, knock.

Who's there?

Thor.

Thor who?

Thor can summon lightning, but Jesus calms the storms!

Anecdote: *Jesus showed His authority over nature by calming the storm with a word.*
Verse: *"He got up, rebuked the wind and said to the waves, 'Quiet! Be still!'" (Mark 4:39)*

Knock, knock.

Who's there?

Harry Potter.

Harry Potter who?

Harry Potter has magic, but Jesus has miracles!

Anecdote: *While Harry uses magic to overcome obstacles, Jesus performed real miracles, including healing the sick.*

Verse: "And Jesus went about all Galilee, teaching in their synagogues, preaching the gospel of the kingdom, and healing all kinds of sickness and all kinds of disease among the people." (Matthew 4:23)

Knock, knock.
Who's there?
Wolverine.
Wolverine who?
Wolverine has claws, but Jesus has the ultimate weapon: love!

Anecdote: *Wolverine uses his powers for battle, while Jesus used love and forgiveness to conquer sin.*
Verse: "But I tell you, love your enemies and pray for those who persecute you." (Matthew 5:44)

Knock, knock.
Who's there?
Superman.
Superman who?
Superman saves the day, but Jesus saves the soul!

Anecdote: *Superman is a symbol of hope, but Jesus offers true salvation and eternal life.*
Verse: "For God so loved the world that he gave his one and only Son, that whoever believes in him shall not perish but have eternal life." (John 3:16)

Knock, knock.

Who's there?
Gandalf.
Gandalf who?
Gandalf may be a wizard, but Jesus is the King of Kings!

Anecdote: *Gandalf fights against evil with wisdom, while Jesus embodies truth and authority over all.*
Verse: *"King of Kings and Lord of Lords." (Revelation 19:16)*

Punny Jokes

Joke: Why did Jesus always carry a map?
Because He wanted to find His way to every lost soul!

Anecdote: *Jesus was known for seeking out those who were lost, both physically and spiritually.*
Verse: *"For the Son of Man came to seek and to save the lost." (Luke 19:10)*

Joke: What did Jesus say to the Marvel superheroes?
"You can have all the powers, but I've got the real superpower: love!"

Anecdote: *Jesus emphasized love as the greatest commandment, even above miraculous abilities.*

Verse: *"Love your neighbor as yourself." (Mark 12:31)*

Joke: Why did Jesus make a great leader?
Because He knew how to handle "cross"-roads!

Anecdote: *Jesus navigated difficult decisions, including His path to the cross with grace and purpose.*
Verse: *"Father, if you are willing, take this cup from me; yet not my will, but yours be done." (Luke 22:42)*

Joke: Why doesn't Jesus need a GPS?
Because He's already the Way!

Anecdote: *Jesus teaches that He is the path to truth and life.*
Verse: *"I am the way and the truth and the life." (John 14:6)*

Joke: What's Jesus' favorite game?
"Hide and Seek," because He loves to find those who are lost!

Anecdote: *Jesus seeks out the lost, just like the shepherd who searches for his sheep.*
Verse: *"Suppose one of you has a hundred sheep and loses one of them." (Luke 15:4)*

Joke: Why did Jesus refuse to play cards?
Because He always "folds" under pressure—into prayer!

Anecdote: *Jesus often withdrew to pray, demonstrating His reliance on God during stressful times.*
Verse: *"But Jesus often withdrew to lonely places and prayed." (Luke 5:16)*

Joke: Why did Jesus invite everyone to dinner?
Because He wanted to "break bread" with sinners!

Anecdote: *Jesus dined with those considered outcasts, showing His willingness to connect with everyone.*
Verse: *"For I have come to call not the righteous, but sinners." (Matthew 9:13)*

Joke: Why did Jesus excel in art class?
Because He could draw a crowd with His stories!

Anecdote: *Jesus used parables to teach profound truths, captivating His audience.*
Verse: *"He taught them many things by parables." (Mark 4:2)*

Joke: What's Jesus' favorite type of music?
"Rock and roll," because He's the rock of our salvation!

Anecdote: *Jesus is often referred to as the cornerstone of faith and salvation.*
Verse: *"The stone the builders rejected has become the cornerstone." (Matthew 21:42)*

Joke: Why did Jesus always win at Monopoly?
Because He knew how to build His "kingdom" without getting kicked out!

Anecdote: *Jesus spoke about the Kingdom of God, illustrating how it grows and thrives through love and grace.*
Verse: *"But seek first his kingdom and his righteousness." (Matthew 6:33)*

One Liner Jokes

Joke: Jesus is like Iron Man—He doesn't need a suit to save the day, just a heart full of love!

Anecdote: *Jesus saved humanity through His love and sacrifice, not technology.*
Verse: *"For God so loved the world that he gave his one and only Son." (John 3:16)*

Joke: When it comes to forgiveness, Jesus is like a Jedi—he uses the Force of love!

Anecdote: *Jesus teaches the importance of forgiving others as a way to reflect God's grace.*
Verse: *"Forgive, and you will be forgiven." (Luke 6:37)*

Joke: Jesus could give Batman a run for his money—He fights evil with love instead of gadgets!

Anecdote: *Jesus confronted sin and evil through compassion rather than weapons.*
Verse: *"But I tell you, love your enemies and pray for those who persecute you." (Matthew 5:44)*

Joke: While Frodo carries the One Ring, Jesus carries the weight of our sins!

Anecdote: Jesus took our sins upon Himself, offering redemption to all.
Verse: "He himself bore our sins in his body on the cross." (1 Peter 2:24)

Joke: Jesus is like Superman—He doesn't wear a cape, but He's still the ultimate savior!

Anecdote: Just as Superman saves people, Jesus came to save all who believe in Him.
Verse: "For the Son of Man came to seek and to save the lost." (Luke 19:10)

Joke: When it comes to overcoming adversity, Jesus is the true wizard—He turns water into wine!

Anecdote: Jesus' first miracle was transforming water into wine at the wedding in Cana, showing His divine power.
Verse: "What Jesus did here in Cana of Galilee was the first of the signs through which he revealed his glory." (John 2:11)

Joke: Jesus doesn't need a magic wand; He just says the word, and miracles happen!

Anecdote: His authority allowed Him to perform countless miracles, showing His divine nature.
Verse: "He healed all the sick." (Matthew 4:24)

Joke: While Captain America stands for justice, Jesus stands for unconditional love!

Anecdote: *Jesus taught that love is the greatest commandment, even surpassing justice.*
Verse: *"Love your neighbor as yourself." (Mark 12:31)*

Joke: Jesus could teach Spiderman a thing or two about "great power" and "great responsibility"!

Anecdote: *Jesus exemplified true responsibility by willingly sacrificing Himself for humanity.*
Verse: *"He laid down his life for us." (1 John 3:16)*

Joke: In the battle of good vs. evil, Jesus doesn't just fight; He redeems!

Anecdote: *Jesus came to offer salvation and healing, transforming lives with His grace.*
Verse: *"The thief comes only to steal and kill and destroy; I have come that they may have life, and have it to the full." (John 10:10)*

Riddle Jokes

Riddle: I can walk on water and calm the sea,

Who am I, can you guess me?
Answer: Jesus!

Anecdote: Jesus demonstrated His power over nature by calming the storm.
Verse: "He got up, rebuked the wind and said to the waves, 'Quiet! Be still!'" (Mark 4:39)

Riddle: I am a carpenter who built a kingdom,
Not with wood, but love and wisdom.
Who am I?
Answer: Jesus!

Riddle: I can turn water into wine,
At a wedding, I did just fine!
Who am I?
Answer: Jesus!

Anecdote: Jesus performed His first miracle at a wedding, showing His compassion for celebration.
Verse: "This, the first of his signs, Jesus performed at Cana in Galilee." (John 2:11)

Riddle: With five loaves and two fish, I fed a crowd,
What miracle is this, can you say it loud?
Answer: The miracle of feeding the 5,000!

Anecdote: Jesus multiplied food to demonstrate His care for people's physical needs.

Verse: *"They all ate and were satisfied." (Luke 9:17)*

Riddle: I walked among sinners, healed the lame,
With my love and mercy, I changed the game.
Who am I?
Answer: Jesus!

Anecdote: *Jesus reached out to those marginalized by society, showcasing His inclusive love.*
Verse: *"For I have come to call not the righteous, but sinners." (Matthew 9:13)*

Riddle: In a garden, I prayed, with sweat like blood,
Who came to betray me with a kiss, not a thud?
Answer: Jesus!

Anecdote: *The agony in the garden highlights Jesus' humanity and His commitment to fulfill His mission.*
Verse: *"Father, if you are willing, take this cup from me." (Luke 22:42)*

Riddle: I raised a friend from death, he was in a tomb,
With just my word, I brought life from gloom.
Who am I?
Answer: Jesus!

Anecdote: *The raising of Lazarus showcased Jesus' power over death and His compassion for friends.*
Verse: *"Lazarus, come out!" (John 11:43)*

Riddle: I am the way, the truth, the life you see,
No one comes to the Father but through me.
Who am I?
Answer: Jesus!

Anecdote: Jesus' declaration highlights His unique role in salvation and relationship with God.
Verse: "I am the way and the truth and the life." (John 14:6)

Riddle: I rode on a donkey, hailed as a king,
Who am I, can you name this thing?
Answer: Jesus!

Anecdote: Jesus' entry into Jerusalem on a donkey fulfilled prophecy and demonstrated His humble kingship.
Verse: "Say to Daughter Zion, 'See, your king comes to you, gentle and riding on a donkey.'" (Matthew 21:5)

Riddle: I rose on the third day, death couldn't hold me,
What is my name, can you see?
Answer: Jesus!

Anecdote: The resurrection is central to Christian faith, affirming Jesus as the conqueror of death.
Verse: "He is not here; he has risen, just as he said." (Matthew 28:6)

Concluding Note

We are reminded as we draw to a conclusion this trip through the life and teachings of Jesus of the great influence His teachings, love, and charity still have on our lives today. Every tale, parable, and miracle gives us a window into His nature as well as a means of getting to know Him better and strengthening our own faith.

We have examined the similarities between Jesus and other fictional characters throughout this book in an effort to elicit thought and humor. These parallels serve as a helpful reminder that Jesus Christ is a magnificent example of all the traits we value in heroes, such as selflessness, forgiveness, and resiliency. His life served as an example of the efficacy of love and the significance of compassion, and it inspires us to abide by these principles.

May you be motivated as you proceed to demonstrate the patience, understanding, and patience that Jesus demonstrated. Allow His lessons to direct your deeds and choices, transforming you into a lighthouse for others. Remind yourself that Jesus is always with you, providing grace and strength to get you through any difficult times.

I am grateful that you have accompanied me on this journey of faith, humor, and exploration. May you share His love and joy with everyone around you by applying the principles you've learned here to every aspect of your life.

Blessings,
Francis Gabriel

Printed in Dunstable, United Kingdom